Monsignor Michael Walsh

GW00645376

THE APPARITION AT KNOCK

A Critical Analysis of Facts and Evidence

THIRD EDITION
ABRIDGED AND UPDATED 2008

VERITAS

First published, 1955
Second edition, 1959
This edition published in 2008 by
Veritas Publications
7/8 Lower Abbey Street
Dublin 1
Ireland
Email publications@veritas.ie
Website www.veritas.ie

ISBN 978 184730 087 4

Scriptural quotation taken from *The Holy Bible*,
Revised Standard Version, Ignatius Press, 1966;
The Navarre Bible, Scepter Publishers, 1999.

Designed by Barbara Croatto

Printed in the Republic of Ireland by Betaprint, Dublin

*Veritas books are printed on paper made from the wood pulp of managed forests. For every tree
felled, at least one tree is planted, thereby renewing natural resources.*

Foreword

The second edition of this book was published in 1959 – three years before the opening of the Second Vatican Council, which held sessions from 1962 to 1965. In the Constitution on the Church (*Lumen Gentium*) the Council enhanced the status of approved apparitions by making a statement on the 'charismatic gifts' … 'bestowed on the People of God by the Holy Spirit'; it declared: 'These charismatic gifts, whether they be the most outstanding or the most simple and widely diffused, are to be received with thanksgiving and consolation, for they are exceedingly suitable and useful for the needs of the Church' (*The Church*, 12).

In this statement, approved apparitions are included among the most outstanding charismatic gifts and are to be received with thanksgiving and consolation.

One of the first developments from this statement of the Council was a less rigid and a more reasonable process for discerning the true from the false apparitions. In the pre-Vatican II era it was sometimes very difficult to provide a definite decision that an apparition was authentic. When the present author was preparing the first edition in 1955, he was aware of what was required and followed the recommended process in Chapter 8. It is a long and detailed chapter, and is more relevant now than it was in 1955, because of the increasing promotion of secularism.

It is recognised that the vast majority of readers are for a long time fully convinced of the authenticity of the apparition; these devout people need not read Chapter 8, except perhaps the last two pages of the chapter where a summary of the findings is given. It may also be said here that in Chapter 16, with the heading, 'The Scriptural Meaning of the Apparition', the character of the apparition is shown to bear in itself the seal of divine origin.

The greater part of the third edition is substantially the same as that contained in the first two editions. Details no longer relevant have been omitted. The story of the Nun of Kenmare in Chapter 11 of the former editions is no longer a chapter; it is shortened to a note at the end of the book. Chapter 10 in former editions is re-written and lengthened in this edition. It is headed 'Other "Apparitions"'. It deals with unsuccessful attempts in 1800 to reproduce the original apparition of 21 August 1879. Chapters 16, 17 and the Appendix are all new.

I wish to express my sincere thanks to Archbishop Michael Neary for writing the preface to this book.

Contents

ACKNOWLEDGEMENTS

*I wish to express my gratitude to the many priests and lay people whom I
consulted, and from whom I received help, when I was seeking information.
I also wish to thank the several priests who offered useful suggestions.
To publishers and owners of copyright, I am grateful for kind permission to use
extracts quoted in this work.
I wish to thank Veritas and editor Caitriona Clarke
for their professional help in preparing this book for publication.*

M.W.

Preface

† Michael Neary, DD, LSS
Archbishop of Tuam

I consider it a privilege to be invited to write the Preface to Monsignor Michael Walsh's book. A native of the neighbouring parish of Aghamore (which was once the united parishes of Aghamore and Knock), Monsignor Walsh has imbibed the history and reverences the mystery of the Apparition throughout his life. In his sixty years as a priest he has ministered to pilgrims in the confessional, has witnessed to and participated in the faith and prayer which attract so many to Our Lady's Shrine. The author is eminently equipped to explain and elucidate the way in which the Apparition so powerfully captures and expresses the central mysteries of our faith. Indeed, the Apparition itself is a succinct but very significant summary of salvation history. The number of pilgrims coming to Knock bears witness to the historical legacy of the Shrine for the faith-life of Irish men and women. Knock has the enduring capacity to touch, inspire and influence people today. In his experience the author is deeply conscious of the way pilgrims from various places with different faith experiences have been drawn to Our Lady's Shrine. The Apparition itself is steeped in a veritable richness of scriptural and theological allusions which the author has so efficiently highlighted.

This book is not only informative and inspirational but also deeply nourishing and supportive of prayerfully pondering.

Central to the Apparition is the Lamb on the altar of sacrifice with the cross in the background. The allusions to the Old

Testament are extremely rich in this regard. The figure of the Lamb is already found in Genesis 22 – when a ram was sacrificed instead of Isaac. We are familiar with the Paschal Lamb in Exodus 12. This lamb was slaughtered and eaten, its blood was put on the doors of the houses when the people were spared. The blood of the sacrificed lamb frees the people.

In Isaiah 53 the figure of the lamb is seen again. Here it is used for the suffering servant who is led 'like a lamb to the slaughter' (Isa 53:7), and 'bore the sin of many, making intercession for the transgressor' (Isa 53:12). These Old Testament figures have already hinted at who Jesus would be. They point to the love of God for us. Jesus is the Lamb who now fulfils and embodies these promises of divine love. The risen Jesus is the Lamb.

The lamb is a central symbol in the Book of the Revelation. The lamb at the Apparition is seen as standing before the cross. Standing is the typical pose of the resurrection. The Lamb of Isaiah 53 was 'slaughtered'. Here the full extent of the love of Jesus is shown. The cross shows the power of his love. Through the cross he becomes fully and forever the Lamb foreshadowed in Genesis, Exodus and Isaiah. Just as in John's Gospel the risen Jesus showed his pierced hands and side to the disciples reminding them of his love (Jn 20:20), so also here, the standing or risen lamb always bears within himself the proof of his redeeming love, the power of his crucifixion. The lamb 'standing as though slain' is the risen Christ.

The Eucharistic theology contained in the Apparition has a very powerful message of the Church today. In the past, dogmatic theology has tended to focus almost exclusively on the Mass as the sacrifice of Calvary re-presented. The liturgical and scriptural renewal of Vatican II placed the emphasis on the meal as we gather around the table of the Lord to partake of the Lamb of God. The juxtaposition in the Apparition of the cross and the lamb underlines the fullness of Eucharistic theology as sacrifice and 'a true banquet in which Christ offers himself as our nourishment' (*Ecclecia De Eucharistia* of Pope John Paul II, para. 16).

The profound relationship between the Church and the Eucharist is underlined by His Holiness, in *Ecclesia De Eucharistia*, Chapter 6, where he describes Mary as 'a woman of the Eucharist in her whole life'. Monsignor Walsh must surely read this as an authentication of his understanding of Mary in the Apparition alongside the altar of sacrifice and the table of the Eucharist.

At Knock the Sacrament of Reconciliation is an integral part of the pilgrimage. Many come to the Shrine to avail of Christ's forgiveness. This is very much in keeping with the centrality of the cross and the lamb in the Apparition. In the fourth Gospel, John the Baptist identifies Jesus as 'the Lamb of God who takes away the sin of the world' (Jn 1:29). The singular of 'sin' (*hamartia*) emphasises the world's collective brokenness, not individual human sins. The expression recalls the servant songs of Second Isaiah (particularly Isa 53:7) or the Passover Lamb, the cultic and liturgical symbol of Israel's deliverance (Ex12:1-13). The early Church quickly interpreted the Passover symbolism in the light of the Eucharist (1 Cor 5:7-8). Indeed, in the fourth Gospel, Jesus' crucifixion is linked to the slaughter of the Paschal Lamb. John's title for Jesus as the Lamb of God draws on a rich heritage of symbols to identify Jesus as the redeemer for the world's sin.

The silent Apparition at Knock, though an embarrassment to some, I believe, has a special significance for a noisy world today as it calls for and challenges us to contemplation.

The author very successfully combines the rich theology of the Apparition with the spirituality which has grown out of it and which is in evidence in the Shrine today. We are very indebted to Monsignor Walsh for the way he introduces us to the extraordinary riches – theological, scriptural, liturgical and spiritual – of the story of Knock, as he invites and encourages us to ponder the mystery and the meaning of this exciting story.

1.

The Faith in Ireland

Ireland's devotion to the Faith is a fact of history. The four hundred years following the coming of St Patrick were so full of glory that they are known as the Golden Age of Irish history. It was an age when Ireland was deservedly renowned for learning and sanctity at home and for great missionary movements abroad. The Golden Age was unhappily ended by a series of invasions and prolonged wars, which in turn were followed by a religious persecution which continued for nearly three hundred years. During the centuries of persecution the Irish people showed their loyalty to the Faith not only by sufferings patiently borne, but by the practice of two great devotions: devotion to the Holy Sacrifice of the Mass and devotion to the Holy Rosary of the Blessed Virgin Mary.

Their endeavours to assist at Mass were reminiscent of the days of the Roman Catacombs. In Ireland, however, the Mass was celebrated above ground in the open air, on a Mass Rock, in some secluded valley. Devotion to the Rosary, practised in the home, made the people familiar with the Mysteries of the Life, Death and Resurrection of Our Saviour, and it fostered a warm devotion to the Mother of God.

Catholic Emancipation came in 1829, but even after that date the Irish people continued to suffer economic misery and destitution. It was estimated that as a result of the Great Famine of the years 1845, 1846 and 1847 over a million people died of hunger and disease, and even a greater number emigrated during the famine years and the years immediately following. Another famine, not as calamitous as the first, occurred in the years 1877, 1878 and 1879. Frequent evictions added to the sufferings of the times. In April 1879 Michael Davitt founded the Land League in Co. Mayo to protect the rights of the tenants and to improve the economic conditions of the people.

In August of that same year 1879 it was reported that Our Lady had appeared to a group of people at Knock, Co. Mayo. The news was received with great enthusiasm by the people in general, and was a consolation to many in their trials. It was perhaps no surprise if Our Lady should show a special honour to Ireland, a country that had been for long ages a shining light in the Church, and whose people had displayed such fervent devotion to the Mass and the Rosary in times of persecution and distress.

2.

Knock and its People in 1879

In 1879 Knock was a small village consisting of a church, two schools and several thatched cottages. The church, the most imposing building in the locality, was cruciform in shape; the nave was about sixty feet in length, and a tower stood at the front entrance. The general appearance of the building, however, was humble. The interior was lit by a few small windows; the floor was roughly flagged; there were few benches. Poor though its appearance was by modern standards, the design at the time of erection was considered ambitious. Built in 1828, the year preceding the passing of the Act of Emancipation, it replaced a thatched building, whose origins would bring one nearer the days of the Mass Rock. Consequently the building erected in 1828, and still standing, marked a definite advance in the progress of the Irish Church since the days of the persecution. A stone in the west wall bears an inscription which, in view of subsequent events, is remarkable:

> Matt II Chap.[1] My house shall be called the House of prayer to all nations. Ps 117. This is the gate of the Lord; the just shall enter into it. Erected by the Rev. P. O'Grady PP 1828.

The tower erected in 1872 was of cut stone, and it introduced an architectural appearance entirely new to the place. In 1878 a great part of the church was wrecked by a storm. The slates were blown off, the windows smashed and the statues of Our Lady, St Joseph and St Aloysius, the only statues in the church, were broken to pieces. The damage having been repaired, two new statues were ordered by the parish priest, but they were broken in transit from the railway station. Two other statues were brought from Lourdes and they arrived safely in the church. One of them was the Statue of Our Lady of Lourdes.

The parish priest, Archdeacon Cavanagh, lived in a thatched cottage of three rooms and a kitchen, situated about one hundred and fifty yards from the church, on the west side of the Claremorris road. After being ordained a priest in 1846, the second year of the great famine, Fr Cavanagh was appointed a curate in Westport, and his first pastoral work was performed in the midst of a starving people. He was appointed parish priest of the combined parishes of Knock and Aghamore in 1867. Eight years later Archbishop McHale appointed him Archdeacon, a title of dignity presupposing outstanding merit and achievement. Amongst the parishioners Archdeacon Cavanagh was reputed a very holy man; he was noted in particular for his devotion to the Immaculate Conception and to the Holy Souls.

The people who lived in the immediate vicinity of the church were simple, hardworking country people, who even in the best of times would not be considered wealthy. In the difficult times of 1879 many of them found it hard to make a living, and so a big proportion of the men of the locality had emigrated to England to earn enough money to support those who were at home. Facing the hard facts of life was the everyday experience of those people. By their work they were close to nature; they had little of the goods of this world, but their faith was strong. No doubt some were more devout than others, but all were faithful members of the Church, and they had a healthy fear of God. In joy and in sorrow the minds of the people and the whole atmosphere of the place were Catholic.

3.

The Apparition at Knock

August 21st, the day before the Octave of the Feast of the Assumption, 1879, was a rainy day in Knock. It does not seem likely there was rain in the early part of the day, as some of the people were working in the meadows that morning; others were bringing turf from the bog. The rain began in a drizzle, probably in the afternoon, and became heavy in the evening. The activities of the people of Knock on that day were ordinary and normal. Mrs Campbell, an old woman, lay sick in her cottage across the road from the church. Her death was expected at any time. Mrs Beirne had just returned from a holiday at the seaside at Lecanvey. A widow, she lived with her family in a cottage in the fields to the east of the church. A local tradition says that Archdeacon Cavanagh had been visiting a distant part of the parish that day, and that when he returned home in the early evening, wet after his journey, he sat at the fire drying his clothes. All things considered, life in Knock on that day, up to evening time, was very much similar to life there on any other wet day. In the evening the apparition was seen. Here we give but a summary of the event recorded. A critical analysis will follow later.

The apparition, according to the evidence, was first seen at about 7.30 p.m. – that is at about nine o'clock summer time, according to modern reckoning. From the official account it appears the first person to notice anything unusual was Margaret Beirne, sister of the sacristan. Shortly after seven o'clock (about

8.30 modern summer time) she had gone to lock the church and on her return saw an unusual brightness over the church, 'but it never entered her head to see or inquire what it was'. She went home and thought no more about it. A short time afterwards Mary McLoughlin, the parish priest's housekeeper, was on her way to visit Mrs Beirne, who had returned that day from her holiday in Lecanvey. To get to the Beirne cottage Mary McLoughlin had to leave the main road and enter a laneway at right angles to the road, and about thirty yards south of the church. On coming opposite the church she saw the figures, but she passed on, and said nothing, thinking 'that possibly the Archdeacon had been supplied with these beautiful figures from Dublin or somewhere else and that he said nothing about them'. She thought 'the whole thing strange', but passed on to Mrs Beirne's house, and mentioned nothing of what she saw. Half an hour later Mary McLoughlin was returning from her visit, and was accompanied by Mrs Beirne's daughter, Mary. When they came near the church gable, Mary Beirne, without having heard anything from Mary McLoughlin, saw the figures, and thinking they were statues asked, 'When did the Archdeacon put the statues at the gable?' Mary McLoughlin, replied, 'He never got them, whoever put them there'. On coming nearer to the gable Mary Beirne exclaimed, 'They are not statues: they are moving. It is the Blessed Virgin'. After some little consultation between the two women, Mary Beirne, feeling quite excited, ran home to tell the others of the wonderful sight – the Blessed Virgin was at the church gable. Mary's brother, Dominick, a young man of about twenty, thought his sister was acting in a very strange way, and did not know what to make of her story. However, Dominick and his mother and his other sister, Margaret, and Dominick's niece, Catherine Murray, all went out, and they too saw the apparition. Mary Beirne, meantime, hurried round to the neighbours living in the immediate vicinity of the church, and told them to come out and see the 'wonderful sight'. Soon a small crowd had gathered at the gable, and they stood gazing at the apparition.

What did they see? According to their own evidence they saw

three figures standing at the gable wall of the church, about eighteen inches, or two feet, above the ground. The central figure was recognised as that of Our Lady. She was wearing a large white cloak fastened at the neck and on her head was a brilliant crown. She held her hands raised to the level of her shoulders and facing each other. Her eyes were raised towards heaven, as if in prayer. She was raised slightly above the other two figures. On Our Lady's right was a figure recognised as that of St Joseph. His hands were joined, his head was slightly bowed and his body slightly bent towards Our Lady, as if paying her his respects. On Our Lady's left was a figure considered by one witness to be St John the Evangelist. He was dressed like a bishop. He held an open book in his left hand, and he had his right hand raised with the index and middle fingers pointing upwards, as if he were preaching and emphasising some special point. On St John's left was an altar, full sized, and on it was a lamb, which was facing towards the figures. Just behind the lamb was a cross. St John was standing in such a position that his back was turned neither to Our Lady nor to the altar, and he was partly facing towards the altar. The altar was in the centre of the gable just under the window on a higher level than the figures; its position was to the east of the figures but in a line slightly behind them. The figures were 'full and round as if they had a body and life', but they spoke no words, and no words were addressed to them. When people approached them, they moved backwards towards the gable. An old woman tried to kiss the feet of Our Lady, but she found nothing in her embrace but the wall. One witness saw a rose on Our Lady's brow and angels hovering round the head of the lamb.

Another said she saw around the lamb a number of stars in the form of a halo. The apparition lasted for about two hours. It was still daylight when it was first seen, but half an hour afterwards darkness had fallen. The three figures and the altar and lamb were surrounded by a soft brilliant light which covered the whole gable of the church. A man who was out on his land half a mile away that night saw the great light over the church. He thought some people must have made a large fire in the church grounds and he wondered why they should have lit it so near the church. He considered the light extraordinary. Rain was falling heavily at the time, and the people standing before the gable were drenched, but no rain fell where the figures were, even though the wind was from the south towards the gable. One witness felt the ground under the figures carefully with her hands and it was perfectly dry.

There were fifteen witnesses of the apparition, but it is known that it was seen by about twenty people altogether. All who came to the church gable saw the apparition. Included in the fifteen were men and women, boys and girls, young and old. The oldest was seventy-five and the youngest was six. When they arrived on the scene first, they exchanged a few words as to the identity of the figures. Then they said prayers, not in common but each in his or her own way. Some of them moved near the figures, but all of them eventually stood motionless gazing at the apparition before them. They were not in ecstasy. All were filled with wonder and amazement, some had warm feelings of devotion, and one at least shed tears of joy. Some of the witnesses stayed an hour and a half, others a shorter time.

After half an hour Mary McLoughlin, the priest's housekeeper, returned to the priest's house. He had been wondering why she had been absent for so long, and when eventually she returned in great excitement, she told him of the wonderful things that were to be seen at the church gable, and suggested that he go out to see them. He considered that perhaps she had seen a reflection of a stained-glass window in the church, took no notice of what she said and did not go out. John Curry and others went away because after being a long time there they were drenched with rain. Judith Campbell departed to attend her sick mother, who had been left alone when news of the apparition was brought. A group was remaining at the church gable until Judith Campbell rushed back to tell them that her mother was dead at her cottage door. Old Mrs Campbell had heard the news that was brought to her house and when she was left alone, she decided that she, too, would go to see the wonderful sight. She was found in a swoon when her daughter arrived. As soon as Judith raised the alarm, all that were still watching the apparition dashed to the old woman. They found that she was not dead. They stayed ten or fifteen minutes until their help was no longer required. They then rushed back to the church gable. When they arrived, there was no apparition to be seen. The rain was dashing on the gable as if nothing unusual had happened. One old woman said she thought the apparition would be there always; the others must have thought likewise. As the wonderful sight was no longer to be seen, all went home.

The following morning the apparition was the talk of the place. The parish priest was told of it when he went to celebrate Mass. He remembered that his housekeeper had told him something of which he took no notice. He questioned the sacristan, Dominick Beirne; he questioned Mary Beirne and others. They all told him their story. Their one regret was that the priest had not seen the apparition. They were convinced that Knock was chosen for the apparition because of the holiness of their priest, and they 'were lost', as they said, because he had not been there.

The news spread quickly. People began to come in crowds to Knock. After some weeks they were coming night and day. Invalids were being carried there, and many extraordinary cures were being claimed. The Archbishop of Tuam at the time was Most Rev. Dr McHale. In October – less than two months after the event – he set up a commission of priests to make an official inquiry into the reported apparition.

4.

Catholic Teaching

Here it may be well to summarise Catholic teaching on the class of supernatural phenomena with which we are dealing, namely, revelations, visions, apparitions.[1]

Divine revelation is a manifestation of a truth by God to man in a manner beyond the ordinary course of nature. Public revelation is addressed to the whole human race. It is contained in the Bible and in Apostolic Tradition. It came to an end with the teaching of the Apostles. The truths of public revelation are all dogmas of the Church, and we are bound to believe them by divine Faith. Private revelation is addressed to an individual or group of individuals for their own welfare or that of others. Instances of private revelation have occurred in every age. Belief in them is not of obligation, even after they have got the approval of the Church. They never become part of Catholic dogma. The revelations made to St Margaret Mary, to St Bernadette at Lourdes and to the children at Fatima are examples of private revelations.

Revelations have been made through visions and apparitions. Neither the word 'vision' nor 'apparition' is always used with exactly the same meaning by all writers. A vision may be described as the apprehension of an image or concept in the psychological genesis of which God has played a special role and for which there is no external correlate present to the beholder. Three kinds of visions are distinguished: intellectual, imaginative and sensible. An intellectual vision is apprehended by the mind alone without an interior image.

St Teresa of Avila had intellectual visions of the Blessed Trinity. An imaginative vision is apprehended by means of an interior image. The image does not give the impression of being exterior. St Paul's vision of Ananias might be described as being an imaginative vision. A sensible vision is also apprehended by means of an interior image, but in such a way as to give the impression of exteriority, and it is related in some way to the external objects present. Instances where Our Lord appeared in the Blessed Eucharist to one person while remaining invisible to all others in the congregation would seem to be examples of sensible visions. Care must be taken not to confuse the imaginative and sensible types of vision with images that are the result of pathological disorder.

An apparition may be described as the manifestation of an external object in a preternatural or supernatural manner. In the subjective sense it is the perception of an external object for whose presence God is in some special way responsible. An apparition is seen by the bodily eyes. The *perception* of an apparition cannot properly be called supernatural, as the senses are acting normally. The appearances of Our Lord after his Resurrection were apparitions. For an apparition to be real and genuine it is not necessary that the object of the apparition be a real human body of flesh and bones. It suffices that it be a sensible or luminous form external to the beholder and occupying a definite space. St Thomas[2] is of the opinion that Our Lord after his Ascension rarely appeared in Person. He discusses appearances of Our Lord in the Blessed Eucharist, and he says these can be explained either as a miraculous impression directly produced in the eye of the beholder, or as a form that is external and visible but distinct from Our Lord's Own Body. The former explanation is adopted if only one person sees the appearance, while others who are present do not see it; the latter, if all present see it. St Thomas reasons in this way, because it is his opinion that the Body of Our Saviour cannot be seen in its own proper form except in the one place which actually contains it. Following this principle some writers are of the opinion that when Our Lady appeared on earth, her body remained in heaven, and what appeared at the spot of the apparition was a visible form which represented her. Writers, however, are not agreed on this point.

God can manifest himself to whomsoever he will, but it is to souls far advanced in holiness that visions *usually* are granted. Fr Poulain says that 'visions and supernatural locutions of a higher order are not usually granted, with any frequency, at least, until the period of ecstasy is almost reached'.[3] The same writer, however, states that 'history proves that visions or exterior locutions have often been received, transiently, at any rate, by persons who were still in the way of ordinary prayer',[4] and that 'experience seems to prove that God has at times manifested himself to simple souls of quite ordinary virtue, in order to found a pilgrimage or to suggest some useful undertaking'.[5] It is recognised that among sinners visions rarely occur.

Accounts of visions or apparitions are not to be accepted without serious examination. There is the possibility of falsehood on the part of the person claiming the vision, or trickery by some other person, or the intervention of the devil, or the supposed vision may be due to illusion or hallucination. It is also possible that mistakes be made in reporting a true revelation. The person who has seen the vision may interpret the message wrongly, or he may unconsciously mingle ideas of his own with what is genuine revelation, or he may subsequently, without realising it, alter parts of the original message. For these reasons the Church insists on careful examination of all accounts of visions and apparitions, and it is well known that she is very slow in giving approval to such accounts.

Even when the Church approves private revelations, she does not make them the object of Catholic Faith. The assent given to them is an act of human faith based on human testimony. Benedict XIV states the mind of the Church thus: 'Although an assent of Catholic faith may not and can not be given to revelations thus approved, still, an assent of human faith, made according to the rules of prudence, is due them; for, according to these rules such revelations are probable and worthy of pious credence.'[6] In giving her approval, the Church simply permits them to be published for the instruction and edification of the faithful.

Many devotions and pilgrimages owe their origin to an apparition. The procedure adopted for deciding on the authenticity of an apparition is that the bishop of the diocese sets up a tribunal to make a thorough investigation of the occurrence. The investigation may take several years. If after careful examination and consultation the bishop finds that the evidence is sufficient to warrant a prudent belief in the authenticity of the apparition, he may make known his decision in the form of an edict. The Bishop of Tarbes declared the authenticity of the apparition at Lourdes in the following manner: 'We judge that Mary Immaculate, Mother of God, has really appeared eighteen times to Bernadette Soubirous, on11 February and the following days, in the Grotto of Massabielle, near the town of Lourdes, and that the apparitions have been proved to be true, and the faithful may believe it in all security.'

The statement of a bishop on the authenticity of an apparition is not, of course, an infallible pronouncement, and does not close the case absolutely. The faithful are not bound by obligation to believe in the apparition, but the verdict of the bishop must be accepted as the decision of an expert, and must be treated with the respect due to the spiritual ruler of the diocese.

At the request of the bishop the Holy See may grant liturgical or other privileges to the shrine, and it may even encourage the devotion or pilgrimage connected with the apparition, but in doing so it acts for theological reasons which are independent of the apparition, and in granting such approval it does not guarantee the historical fact of the apparition. In 1877 the Congregation of Rites was asked whether it approved the apparitions at Lourdes and La Salette. The reply was: 'Such apparitions are neither approved nor reproved or condemned by the Holy See; they are simply authorised as pious beliefs on purely human faith, according to a tradition which has been confirmed by suitable testimonies and evidences.'[7]

In general it can be said that until such time as a decision has been made by competent authority, two extremes are to be avoided in regard to reported revelations and apparitions. One is the credulous mentality which accepts all such stories uncritically. The other is the frame of mind which automatically rejects them. Neither attitude is scientific. Care must be taken to find the truth. True revelations are useful. They are the work not only of God's power, but of his wisdom. In making revelations and manifesting apparitions God uses extraordinary means to achieve extraordinary good.

Approved apparitions have been given an enhanced status by the Second Vatican Council (1962–1965). In its Constitution on the Church (*Lumen Gentium*) the Council refers to charismatic gifts bestowed on the People of God by the Holy Spirit: 'These charismatic gifts, whether they be the most outstanding or the most simple and widely diffused, are to be received with thanksgiving and consolation, for they are exceedingly suitable and useful for the needs of the Church.' (*The Church*, 12).

Apparitions are most outstanding gifts.

5.

The 1879 Commission

In October 1879 the Archbishop of Tuam, Most Rev. Dr MacHale, set up a commission of three priests to hold an inquiry into the reported apparition at Knock.[1] The members of the commission were Archdeacon Cavanagh, Parish Priest, Knock; Canon Waldron, Parish Priest, Ballyhaunis, and Canon Ulick Bourke, Parish Priest, Claremorris. According to the *Weekly News*[2] the following priests, at the request of the Archdeacon, assisted the commission in its proceedings: Rev. James Corbett, CC, Claremorris; Rev. Michael O'Donoghue, CC, Ballyhaunis; Rev. Michael · Heaney, CC, Aughamore; Rev. Michael Curran, CC, Claremorris; Rev. James Killeen, CC, Crossboyne; and Rev. Father McAlpine, CC, Ballindine.

The original documents of this commission are not extant. We know from reliable contemporary records that the commission examined fifteen witnesses, and took a deposition from each.[3] The witnesses were not sworn. The *Weekly News,* whose representative interviewed Archdeacon Cavanagh, states that the commission sat for one day only in the sacristy of the church at Knock and personally examined every witness.[4]

There are two versions of the depositions taken. One was first published by John MacPhilpin in the *Tuam News* in January 1880. These newspaper articles were prepared by John MacPhilpin and published by Gill & Son in March 1880 in the booklet *The Apparitions and Miracles at Knock.* The newspaper articles of

January 1880 are not extant. The other version of the depositions was given in the *Weekly News* February 1880, and reprinted along with other *Weekly News* articles of 1880 by T.D. Sullivan in a booklet called *Apparitions at the Church of Knock*.[5] The difference between the two versions are of little consequence. Only twelve of the fifteen statements are given by T.D. Sullivan. Those twelve in both versions tell the same story with even verbal agreement in many places. The *Weekly News* version is longer and less ordered in composition than that given by MacPhilpin. The MacPhilpin version shows traces of the literary embellishment of an editor. It is obvious that neither version is the verbatim record of the inquiry. The statements in both versions give a continuous story, whereas there must have been much questioning to elicit all the details given. Second, many of the words and forms of expression in both versions must have been supplied by the commission, as ordinary country people would not have had such a vocabulary and facility of expression at their disposal. It is actually stated in a bracketed note in one of the MacPhilpin depositions that the witness did not know the words for certain details he was describing. The words in that case, certainly, and, we may presume, elsewhere too, were supplied by one or other of the priests.

The MacPhilpin version enjoys the greater authority: indeed, one might say it has been followed by all, or nearly all, writers from 1880 to the present time. John MacPhilpin was nephew of Canon Ulick Bourke and proprietor of the *Tuam News*, a local paper founded some years previously by Canon Bourke. Uncle and nephew had cooperated for years in the work of the paper. In publishing the evidence MacPhilpin gave the depositions as the official depositions of the commission. We can take it that the depositions published by him would have been supplied to him by his uncle, who was secretary of the commission, and that they are a faithful rendering of the evidence given by the witnesses. Furthermore MacPhilpin lived in the Archbishop's own parish of Tuam; one might say the booklet was published under the very eyes of the Archbishop; it had wide circulation in the diocese. His claim to be giving the evidence of the commission was never denied, as far as we know. Had it been denied, it would without doubt be widely known. A second edition of the booklet was published in 1894; the depositions in this second edition are given exactly as in the 1880 edition. Before a formal commission set up in 1936 several people from Knock testified that the account of the apparition they heard from eyewitnesses agreed with the published accounts. MacPhilpin's book was read in Knock. Most important of all, in 1936 the surviving witnesses confirmed on oath the depositions attributed to them by MacPhilpin, making some changes that did not affect the authenticity of MacPhilpin's records. The 1936 Commission accepted the depositions given by MacPhilpin as being an authentic copy of the originals.

While the depositions are not a verbatim report, it will be conceded that in them the witnesses, at least the principal ones, speak in character. Patrick Hill speaks true to type as a boy of thirteen. His sentences are short and animated. He is the first of the group to cross the wall. He has no inhibitions about going right up to the figures, so that he may see everything and miss nothing. He is observant; he sees details that others do not see.

The evidence of Mrs Trench, who was 'three score and fifteen years', has its own characteristic charm. It is to be regretted that her story as told in Irish was not preserved in that tongue. But even the translation reflects the piety and devotion typical of an old Irish woman. Her first act was to throw herself on her knees and give thanks; she tried to embrace the feet of Our Lady; she was so taken up with Our Lady that she did not pay much attention to the others. She could think of nothing else while there but giving thanks to God and repeating her prayers.

The wealth of detail given not only shows that the witnesses must have been subjected to close questioning, but also that the questioner or questioners were fully aware of the possible natural explanations for the occurrence; the details sought and given are not just haphazard. They supply information that is necessary for determining the nature of the apparition, and such as would be sought by an enlightened critic. It is clear, therefore, that even though the depositions are not a verbatim report, they are nevertheless reliable.

In the next chapter we reproduce the evidence as given by John MacPhilpin in *The Apparitions and Miracles at Knock*. The introduction to the evidence, the note after Mary McLoughlin's statement and the note at the end of the spelling of the name 'Byrne' are also taken from MacPhilpin.

6.

The Evidence of the 1879 Commission

Depositions taken in the presence of the Very Rev. Archdeacon Bartholomew A. Cavanagh, PP; of Rev. James Canon Waldron, PP, Ballyhaunis; and Rev. U.J. Canon Bourke, PP, of Kilcolman, Claremorris, Co. Mayo, deputed by His Grace, the Archbishop of Tuam, to see into the truth of the vision alleged to have appeared at the Catholic church of Knock on the evening of 21 August, the octave of the Assumption of the BVM, 1879.

First Witness
Testimony of Patrick Hill

I am Patrick Hill; I live in Claremorris; my aunt lives at Knock; I remember the 21 August last; on that day I was drawing home turf, or peat, from the bog, on an ass. While at my aunt's at about eight o'clock in the evening, Dominick Beirne came into the house; he cried out: Come up to the chapel and see the miraculous lights, and the beautiful visions that are to be seen there. I followed him; another man, by name Dominick Beirne, and John Durkan, and a small boy named John Curry, came with me; we were all together; we ran over towards the chapel. When we, running south-west, came so far from the village that on our turning the gable came in view, we immediately beheld the lights, a clear, white light, covering most of the gable, from the ground up to the window and higher. It was a kind of changing bright light, going sometimes up high and again not so high. We saw the figures – the Blessed Virgin, St Joseph and St John, and an altar, with the Lamb on the altar, and a cross behind the Lamb. At this time we reached as far as the wall fronting the gable; there were other people there before me; some of them were praying, some not; all were looking at the vision; they were leaning over the wall or ditch, with their arms resting on the top. I saw the figures and brightness; the boy John Curry, from behind the wall, could not see them; but I did; and he asked me to lift him up till he could see the grand babies, as he called the figures; it was raining; some – amongst them Mary McLoughlin – who beheld what I now saw, had gone away; others were coming.

After we prayed a while I thought it right to go across the wall and into the chapel yard. I brought little Curry with me; I went then up closer; I saw everything distinctly. The figures were full and round, as if they had a body and life; they said nothing, but as we approached, they seemed to go back a little towards the gable. I distinctly beheld the Blessed Virgin Mary, life size, standing about two feet or so above the ground, clothed in white robes, which were fastened at the neck; her hands were raised to the height of the shoulders, as if in prayer, with the palms facing one another, but slanting inwards towards the face; the palms were not turned towards the people, but facing each other as I have described; she appeared to be praying; her eyes were turned, as I saw, towards heaven; she wore a brilliant crown on her head, and over the forehead, where the crown fitted the brow, a beautiful rose; the crown appeared brilliant, and of a golden brightness, of a deeper hue, inclined to a mellow yellow, than the striking whiteness of the robes she wore; the upper parts of the crown appeared to be a series of sparkles, or glittering crosses. I saw her eyes, the balls, the pupils, and the iris of each – [the boy did not know those special names of those parts of the eye, but he pointed to them, and described them in his own way]

– I noticed her hands especially, and face; her appearance; the robes came only as far as the ankles; I saw the feet and the ankles; one foot, the right, was slightly in advance of the other; at times she appeared, and all the figures appeared to move out and again to go backwards; I saw them move; she did not speak; I went up very near; one old woman went up and embraced the Virgin's feet and she found nothing in her arms or hands; they receded, she said, from her; I saw St Joseph to the Blessed Virgin's right hand; his head was bent, from the shoulders, forward; he appeared to be paying his respects; I noticed his whiskers; they appeared slightly grey; there was a line or dark mearing between the figure of the Blessed Virgin and that of St Joseph, so that one could know St Joseph, and the place where his figure appeared distinctly from that of the Blessed Virgin, and the spot where she stood. I saw the feet of St Joseph, too; his hands were joined like a person at prayer. The third figure that stood before me was that of St John the Evangelist; he stood erect to the Gospel side of the altar and at an angle with the figure of the Blessed Virgin, so that his back was not turned to the altar, nor to the Mother of God; his right arm was at an angle with a line drawn across from St Joseph to where Our Blessed Lady appeared to be standing; St John was dressed like a bishop preaching; he wore a small mitre on his head; he held a Mass book, or a Book of the Gospels, in the left hand; the right hand was raised to the elevation of the head; while he kept the index finger and the middle finger of the right hand raised, the other three fingers of the same hand were shut; he appeared as if he were preaching but I heard no voice; I came so near, that I looked into the book; I saw the lines and the letters. St John wore no sandals; his left hand was turned towards the altar that was behind him; the altar was a plain one, like any ordinary altar, without any ornaments. On the altar stood a Lamb – the size of a lamb eight weeks old; the face of the Lamb was fronting the west, and looking in the direction of the Blessed Virgin and St Joseph; behind the Lamb a large cross was placed erect or perpendicular on the altar; around the Lamb I saw angels hovering during the whole time, for the space of one hour and a half or longer; I saw their wings fluttering, but I did not perceive their heads or faces, which were not turned to me. For the space of one hour and a half we were under the pouring rain; at this time I was very wet: I noticed that the rain did not wet the figures which appeared before me, although I was wet myself; I went away then.

(Signed) Patrick Hill
Witness present – U.J. Canon Bourke
8 October 1879

* * *

Second Witness
Testimony of Mary McLoughlin
I, Mary McLoughlin, live in Knock; I am housekeeper to the Rev. Archdeacon Cavanagh; I remember the evening of 21 August; at the hour of seven or so, or a little later, while it was yet a bright day, I passed from the Rev. Archdeacon's house on by the chapel, towards the house of a Mrs Beirne, widow. On passing by the chapel, and at a little distance from it, I saw a wonderful number of strange figures or appearances at the gable, one like the BV Mary, and one like St Joseph, another a bishop; I saw an altar; I was wondering to see there such an extraordinary group; yet I passed on and said nothing, thinking that possibly the Archdeacon had been supplied with these beautiful figures from Dublin, or somewhere else, and that he said nothing about them, but had left them in the open air; I saw a white light about them; I thought the whole thing strange; after looking at them I passed on to the house of Mrs Beirne's in the village; after reaching Widow Beirne's house I stayed there half an hour at least; I returned then

homewards to the Archdeacon's house, accompanied by Miss Mary Beirne, and as we approached the chapel, she cried out, 'Look at the beautiful figures'. We gazed on them for a little, and then I told her to go for her mother, widow Beirne, and her brother and her sister, and her niece, who were still in the house which she and I had left. I remained looking at the sight before me until the mother, sister and brother of Miss Mary Beirne came; at the time I was outside the ditch and to the south-west of the schoolhouse near the road, about thirty yards or so from the church; I leaned across the wall in order to see, as well as I could, the whole scene. I remained now for the space of at least a quarter of an hour, perhaps longer. I told Miss Beirne then to go for her uncle, Bryan Beirne, and her aunt, Mrs Bryan Beirne, or any of the neighbours whom she should see, in order that they might witness the sight that we were then enjoying. It was now about a quarter past eight o'clock, and beginning to be quite dark. The sun had set; it was raining at the time. I beheld, on this occasion, not only the three figures, but an altar further on the left of the figure of the BVM, and to the left of the bishop and above the altar a lamb about the size of that which is five weeks old. Behind the Lamb appeared the cross; it was away a bit from the Lamb, while the latter stood in front from it, and not resting on the wood of the cross. Around the Lamb a number of gold-like stars appeared in the form of a halo. This altar was placed right under the window of the gable and more to the east of the figures, all, of course, outside the church at Knock.

I parted from the company or gathering at eight and a half o'clock. I went to the priest's house and told what I had beheld, and spoke of the beautiful things that were to be seen at the gable of the chapel; I asked him, or said, rather, it would be worth his while to go to witness them. He appeared to make nothing of what I said, and consequently he did not go. Although it was pouring rain, the wall had a bright, dry appearance, while the rest of the building appeared to be dark.

I did not return to behold the visions again after that, remaining at my house. I saw the sight for fully an hour. Very Rev. B. Cavanagh heard the next day all about the apparition from the others who had beheld it; and then it came to his recollection that I had told him the previous evening about it, and asked him to see it.

Note: Mary McLoughlin had gone away before Patrick Hill came. Their testimony relates to two distinct and separate times while the apparition was present. She saw it, like one who did not care to see it, and in a transverse direction, not straight; he saw it directly and fully, and like a confiding child, went up calmly to where the Blessed Virgin stood.

* * *

Third Witness
Testimony of Mary Beirne, aged about twenty-six years
I live in the village of Knock, to the east side of the chapel; Mary McLoughlin came on the evening of 21 August to my house at about half-past seven o'clock; she remained some little time; I came back with her as she was returning homewards; it was eight o'clock or a quarter to eight at the time. It was still bright; I had never heard from Miss McLoughlin about the vision which she had seen just before that. The first I learned of it was on coming at the time just named from my mother's house in company with Miss Mary McLoughlin, and, at the distance of three hundred yards or so from the church, I beheld, all at once, standing out from the gable, and rather to the west of it, three figures which, on more attentive inspection, appeared to be that of the Blessed Virgin, of St Joseph and St John. That of the Blessed Virgin was life-size, the others apparently either not so big or not so high as her figure; they stood a little distance out from the gable wall, and, as well as I could judge, a foot and a half or

two feet from the ground. The Virgin stood erect, with eyes raised to heaven, her hands elevated to the shoulders or a little higher, the palms inclined slightly towards the shoulders or bosom. She wore a large cloak of a white colour, hanging in full folds and somewhat loosely around her shoulders, and fastened to the neck; she wore a crown on the head – rather a large crown – and it appeared to me somewhat yellower than the dress or robes worn by our Blessed Lady. In the figure of St Joseph the head was slightly bent, and inclined towards the Blessed Virgin, as if paying her respect; it represented the saint as somewhat aged, with grey whiskers and greyish hair. The third figure appeared to be that of St John the Evangelist; I do not know, only I thought so, except the fact that at one time I saw a statue at the chapel of Lecanvey, near Westport, Co. Mayo, very much resembling the figure which stood now before me in group with St Joseph and Our Blessed Lady, which I beheld on this occasion. He held the Book of Gospels, or the Mass Book, open in his left hand, while he stood slightly turned on the left side towards the altar that was over a little from him. I must remark that the statue which I had formerly seen at Lecanvey chapel had no mitre on its head, while the figure which I now beheld had one – not a high mitre, but a short-set kind of one. The statue at Lecanvey had a book in the left hand, and the fingers of the right hand raised. The figure before me on this present occasion of which I am speaking had a book in the left hand, as I have stated, and the index finger and the middle finger of the right hand raised, as if he were speaking, and impressing some point forcibly on an audience. It was this coincidence of figure and pose that made me surmise, for it is only an opinion, that the third figure was that of St John, the beloved disciple of Our Lord. But I am not in any way sure what saint or character the figure represented. I said, as I now expressed, that it was St John the Evangelist, and then all the others present said the same – said what I stated. The altar was under the window, which is in the gable, and a little to the west near the centre, or a little beyond it. Towards this altar St John – as I shall call the figure – was looking, while he stood at the Gospel side of the said altar, with his right arm inclined at an angle outwardly, towards the Blessed Virgin. The altar appeared to me to be like the altars in use in the Catholic church – large and full-sized. It had no linens, no candles, nor any special ornamentations; it was only a plain altar. Above the altar, and resting on it was a Lamb, standing with the face towards St John, thus fronting the western sky. I saw no cross nor crucifix. On the body of the Lamb, and around it, I saw golden stars, or small brilliant lights, glittering like jets or glass balls, reflecting the light of some luminous body. I remained from a quarter past eight to half-past nine o'clock. At the time it was raining.

* * *

Fourth Witness
Testimony of Patrick Walsh, aged sixty-five years
My name is Patrick Walsh; I live at Ballinderrig, an English mile from the chapel at Knock. I remember well the 21 August 1879. It was a very dark night. It was raining heavily. About nine o'clock on that night I was going on some business through my land, and standing a distance of about half a mile from the chapel, I saw a very bright light in the southern gable-end of the chapel; it appeared to be a large globe of golden light; I never saw, I thought, so brilliant a light before; it appeared high up in the air above and around the chapel gable, and it was circular in its appearance: it was quite stationary, and it seemed to retain the same brilliancy all through. The following day I made inquiries in order to learn if there were any lights seen in the place that night; it was only then I heard of the Vision or Apparition that the people had seen.

Fifth Witness
Testimony of Patrick Beirne, son of the Elder Patrick Beirne, of Knock

I am sixteen years of age; I live quite near the chapel; I remember well the evening of 21 August; it was Thursday, the evening before the Octave day. Dominick Beirne, Jr, a namesake of mine, came to my house and said that he had seen the biggest sight that ever he witnessed in his life. It was then about eight o'clock. I came by the road on the west side of the church. I saw the figures clearly, fully, and distinctly – the Blessed Virgin, St Joseph and that of a bishop, said to be St John the Evangelist. Young Beirne then told what he saw regarding the Vision, just as it had been described already by several persons who were present. The young fellow showed by his hands and position how the image or apparition of the Blessed Virgin Mary and that of St Joseph and St John stood.

I remained only ten minutes, and then I went away. All this happened between a quarter or so past eight o'clock and half-past nine.

* * *

Sixth Witness
Testimony of Margaret Beirne, Widow of Dominick Beirne, of Knock

I, Margaret Beirne, nee Bourke, widow of Dominick Beirne, live near the chapel at Knock. I remember the evening of 21 August. I was called out at about a quarter past eight o'clock by my daughter Margaret to see the Vision of the Blessed Virgin Mary, and of the saints who appeared at the end of the little church; it was getting dark; it was raining. I came with others to the wall opposite the gable; I saw then and there distinctly the three images – one of the Blessed Virgin Mary, one of St Joseph, and the third, as I learned, that of St John the Evangelist. I saw an altar, too, and a Lamb on it, somewhat whiter than the altar. I did not see the cross on the altar. The Blessed Virgin Mary appeared in the attitude of prayer, with her eyes turned up towards heaven, a crown on her head, and an outer garment thrown round her shoulders. I saw her feet. St Joseph appeared turned towards the Blessed Virgin, with head inclined. I remained looking on for fully fifteen minutes; then I left, and returned to my own house.

* * *

Seventh Witness
Testimony of Dominick Beirne
I am brother of Mary Beirne, who has given her evidence already; I live near the chapel of Knock; my age is twenty years. On the occasion when my sister came at about eight o'clock on the evening of 21 August into our house, she exclaimed: 'Come, Dominick, and see the image of the Blessed Virgin, as she has appeared to us down at the chapel.' I said, 'What image?' and then she told me, as she has already described it for Your Reverence in her testimony; she told me all she was after seeing; I then went with her, and by this time some ten or twelve people had been collected around the place, namely, around the ditch or wall fronting the gable, where the vision was being seen, and to the south of the schoolhouse; then I beheld the three likenesses or figures that have been already described – the Blessed Virgin, St Joseph, St John, as my sister called the bishop, who was like one preaching, with his hands raised towards the shoulder, and the forefinger and middle finger pointedly set; the other two fingers compressed by the thumb; in his left he held a book; he was so turned that he looked half towards the altar and half towards the people; the eyes of the images could be seen; they were like figures, in as much as they did not speak. I was filled with wonder at the sight I saw. I was so affected that I shed tears; I continued looking on for fully an hour, and then I

went away to visit Mrs Campbell, who was in a dying state; when we returned the Vision had disappeared.

* * *

Eighth Witness
Mrs Hugh Flatley, widow of Hugh Flatley, states:
I was passing by the chapel of Knock, on the evening of 21 August, about eight o'clock, and I beheld most clearly and distinctly the figures of the Blessed Virgin Mary, St Joseph and that of St John the Evangelist, standing erect at the gable end of the chapel, towards the south side; I thought that the parish priest had been ornamenting the church, and got some beautiful likenesses removed outside.

* * *

Ninth Witness
Testimony of Bridget Trench, aged seventy-five (three score and fifteen) years
The testimony of this witness was given in the Irish language. Her words were translated by Fr Corbett into English while she spoke. The following is the version of what she said:
My name is Bridget Trench; I live near the chapel of Knock. About half-past seven o'clock on the night of 21 August I was in the house of Mrs Campbell, which is quite near to the chapel; while I was there Mary Beirne came in and said there was a sight to be seen at the chapel such as she never before beheld, and she told us all to come and see it; I asked her what it was, and she said that the Blessed Virgin, St Joseph and St John were to be seen there. I went out immediately and came to the spot indicated. When I arrived there I saw distinctly the three figures. I threw myself on my knees and exclaimed: 'A hundred thousand thanks to God and to the glorious Virgin that has given us this manifestation.' I went in

immediately to kiss, as I thought, the feet of the Blessed Virgin; but I felt nothing in the embrace but the wall, and I wondered why I could not feel with my hands the figures which I had so plainly and so distinctly seen. The three figures appeared motionless, statue-like; they were standing by the gable of the church in the background, and seemed raised about two feet above the ground. The Blessed Virgin was in the centre; she was clothed in white, and covered with what appeared one white garment; her hands were raised to the same position as that in which a priest holds his hands when praying at holy Mass.

I remarked distinctly the lower portions of her feet, and kissed them three times; she had on her head something resembling a crown, and her eyes were turned up heavenwards. I was so taken with the Blessed Virgin that I did not pay much attention to any other; yet I saw also the two other figures – St Joseph standing to the right of the Blessed Virgin, or to the left, as I looked at him, his head bent towards her and his hands joined; and the other figure, which I took to be St John the Evangelist, was standing at her left. I heard those around me say that the image was St John. It was raining very heavily at the time, but no rain fell where the figures were. I felt the ground carefully with my hands, and it was perfectly dry. The wind was blowing from the south, right against the gable of the chapel, but no rain fell on that portion of the gable or chapel in which the figures were. There was no movement or active sign of life about the figures, and I could not say whether they were what living beings would in their place appear to be or not; but they appeared to me so full and so life-like and so life-size that I could not understand why I could not feel them with my hands such as I beheld them with my eyes. There was an extraordinary brightness about the whole gable of the chapel, and it was observed by several who were passing along the road at the time. I remained there altogether about an hour, and when I came there first I thought I would never leave it. I would not have gone so soon as I did, but that I considered that the figures and the brightness would continue there always, and that on coming back I would again behold them. I continued to repeat the Rosary on my beads while there, and I felt great delight and pleasure in looking at the Blessed Virgin. I could think of nothing else while there but giving thanks to God and repeating my prayers.

* * *

Tenth Witness
Testimony of Catherine Murray, a girl of about eight years and six months, grand-daughter of Mrs Beirne
I am living at Knock; I was staying at my grandmother's. I followed my aunt and uncle to the chapel; I then saw the likeness of the Blessed Virgin Mary and that of St Joseph and St John, as I learned from those that were around about where I was; I saw them all for fully twenty minutes or thirty minutes.

* * *

Eleventh Witness
Testimony of John Curry, a young boy, about six years old
The child says he saw the images – beautiful images – the Blessed Virgin and St Joseph. He could state no more than that he saw the fine images and the light, and heard the people talk of them, and went upon the wall to see the nice things and the lights.

* * *

Twelfth Witness
Testimony of Judith Campbell of Knock
I live at Knock; I remember the evening and night of 21 August last. Mary Beirne called at my house about eight o'clock on that evening, and asked me to come to see the great sight at the chapel. I went up with her to the place, and I saw outside the chapel, at the gable of the sacristy facing the south, three figures representing St Joseph, St John and the Blessed Virgin Mary; also an altar, and the likeness of a Lamb on it, with a cross at the back of the Lamb. I saw a most beautiful crown on the brow or head of the Blessed Virgin. Our Lady was in the centre of the group, a small height above the other two; St Joseph to her right, and bent towards the Virgin; St John, as we were led to call the third figure, was to the left of the Virgin, and in his left hand he held a book; his right was raised with the first and second fingers closed, and the forefinger and middle finger extended as if he were teaching. The night came on, and it was very wet and dark; there was a beautiful light shining around the figures or likenesses that we saw. I went within a foot of them; none of us spoke to them; we believed they were St Joseph and St John the Evangelist, because some years ago statues of St Joseph and of the Evangelist were in the chapel at Knock. All the figures were in white, or in a robe of silver-like whiteness; St John wore a small mitre. Though it was raining, the place in which the figures appeared was quite dry.

Note: There was no statute of St John the Evangelist in Knock before the apparition. The witness was mistaken in this. – M.W.

* * *

Thirteenth Witness
Testimony of Margaret Beirne
I, Margaret Beirne, live near Knock chapel; I am sister to

Mary Beirne who has seen the vision; I remember the night of 21 August; I left my own house at half-past seven o'clock, and went to the chapel and locked it. I came out to return home; I saw something luminous or bright at the south gable, but it never entered my head that it was necessary to see or inquire what it was; I passed by and went home. Shortly after, about eight o'clock, my niece, Catherine Murray, called me out to see the Blessed Virgin and the other saints that were standing at the south gable of the chapel. I went out then, and ran up to see what was to be seen. I there beheld the Blessed Virgin with a bright crown on her head, and St Joseph to her right, his head inclined a little towards Our Blessed Lady, and St John the Evangelist to her left, eastward, holding in his left hand a book of the Gospels, and his right hand raised the while, as if in the attitude of preaching to the people who stood before him at the ditch. The Virgin appeared with hands uplifted as in prayer, with eyes turned towards heaven, and wearing a lustrous crown; I saw an altar there; it was surrounded with a bright light, nay, with a light at times sparkling, and so too were the other figures, which were similarly surrounded.

* * *

Fourteenth Witness
Testimony of Dominick Beirne (Senior)
I live at Knock; I remember the evening of 21 August; my cousin, Dominick Beirne, came to see us at about eight o'clock p.m., and called me to see the vision of the Blessed Virgin Mary and other saints at the south gable of the chapel. I went with him. When I reached the south side of the chapel, we saw the image of the Blessed Virgin Mary, having her hands uplifted, and her eyes turned up towards heaven, as if in prayer, and she was dressed in a white cloak. To her right I saw St Joseph, and on her left St John, just as the other persons

had told me before I came. I saw an altar there, and figures representing saints and angels traced or carved on the lower part of it. The night was dark and raining, and yet these images, in the dark night, appeared with bright lights as plain as under the noon-day sun. At the time it was pitch dark and raining heavily, and yet there was not one drop of rain near the images. There was a mitre on St John's head, nearly like to that which a bishop wears. I was there only for one quarter of an hour. At the time I was there, five other persons were in it with me, looking on at the apparition. All the figures appeared clothed in white; the whiskers on St Joseph were in iron grey; the Blessed Virgin had on a white cloak. The reason I had for calling the third figure St John is because some saw his statue or his likeness at Lecanvey parish chapel.

* * *

The **Fifteenth Witness** is *John Durkan*, one of the three who accompanied young Hill. His testimony is the same as that given by each of the Beirnes.

NOTE: The Beirne family spell their name Beirn, or Beirne; correspondents spell the name 'BYRNE', which is in sound the same.

7.

The Findings of the Commission

Of the three members of the commission the most distinguished was Canon Ulick Bourke. He was a man of keen intellect and unusual literary ability. As a student in Second Divinity in Maynooth he had published *The College Irish Grammar.* After Ordination he was appointed to St Jarlath's College, Tuam, where he spent twenty years – thirteen as president. He was the author of several books; founded the newspaper, the *Tuam News,* and was elected a member of the Royal Irish Academy. In 1878 he was appointed parish priest of Claremorris.

Canon Waldron was parish priest in Ballyhaunis. Of the three he was least known. He had a reputation in the diocese as a theologian of some merit.

Archdeacon Cavanagh was parish priest of Knock. He was known as a very saintly priest. It is urged against him that he was credulous – that he was himself a visionary. There is no evidence that he ever claimed to have seen visions before the apparition of 1879. He refused to believe the first account he heard of the apparition. It is certain, however, that he claimed to have seen visions in 1880 and afterwards.

The *Weekly News* mentions the names of several other priests who were invited by Archdeacon Cavanagh to assist the commission in its investigations. In a published interview[1] Mrs O'Connell (nee Mary Beirne) told how her evidence was taken in 1879 by the commissioners, and that a fortnight later twenty more priests arrived and carried out elaborate tests with magic lantern slides. It is worthy of note that the 1936 commission produced the interview just mentioned in examining Mrs O'Connell. She confirmed it, but made the correction that her evidence in 1879 was taken by three priests, not two, as stated in the published account, and she named the three members of the commission. MacPhilpin makes no mention of the other priests said to have been invited by Archdeacon Cavanagh. But from him we gather that Fr Corbett, CC, Claremorris, was present at the hearing of at least one witness. He states in a note that Bridget Trench gave her evidence in the Irish language, and that it was translated into English by Fr Corbett while she spoke.

The *Weekly News* gives us to understand that the report of the commission was sent to the Archbishop before Archdeacon Cavanagh started his diary of cures, and it says that this diary was opened on 31 October 1879. MacPhilpin does not mention on what date the report was submitted, but he states definitely that it was submitted, and his booklet was published in March 1880. The commission therefore began its investigation on 8 October and its report was submitted possibly before the end of the month and certainly before the following March. The time taken by the commission to deliberate on the evidence before coming to a decision may seem to be short. In deciding the length of time that should be taken it is not entirely apposite to compare it with the length of time taken by similar tribunals investigating other apparitions. It is to be decided rather by the nature of the facts and the evidence in each particular case. The task confronting the Knock Commission was much simpler and less formidable than that of other similar commissions on the Continent. In Lourdes, for instance, there was only one witness, and she was a child. At La Salette there were two witnesses, who were children, and at Fatima the witnesses were three children. Psychologists and others distrust, for valid reasons, children's stories about the supernatural. A child's story of an apparition has to be subjected to very rigorous tests before being accepted as reliable. At Knock the number of witnesses was at least fifteen, the majority of whom were adults; there were some children amongst them, but they were not the first to see the apparition. Second, even though large crowds were present during most of the apparitions at Lourdes and Fatima, nobody could see the apparition except Bernadette at Lourdes, and the three children at Fatima. At Knock, all who were present saw the apparition. Third, in many other apparitions the witness or witnesses had ecstatic experience. This in some way added to the complexity of the investigators' work. At Knock there was no experience of ecstasy. The reactions of the witnesses were normal.

There was awe, wonder, excitement; there was devotion too, but not of an extraordinary kind. The story of the witnesses was straightforward, objective and substantiated by a super-abundance of eyewitness evidence. Accordingly, the work before the Knock commission was comparatively simple, and would not require all the elaborate processes adopted elsewhere. The time required, therefore, for coming to a decision on the apparition at Knock could be notably less than the time taken by other similar tribunals, and a reasoned judgement could be arrived at within a month.

The statement of the *Weekly News* that the commission sat for one day only in the sacristy of the church can refer only to the session at which they took the evidence. It is reasonable to infer that they had other meetings for deliberation. We know that about a fortnight after the taking of the evidence Dr Lennon of Maynooth carried out his test. He was invited to do so by the commission. The occasion was obviously considered one of special moment, as Mrs O'Connell says there were twenty priests present. It is certain that the commission requested the advice of Dr Lennon, as Dr Lennon later wrote a letter to Archdeacon Cavanagh, in which 'at the request of the commission' he gives a statement of his opinion.[2] The tests and the letter show that the commission's investigations continued after the taking of evidence.

Dr Lennon's letter is dated 'Feast of Our Lady of Mount Carmel'. The year is not stated. It could not have been 1879, as the Feast of Our Lady of Mount Carmel occurs on 16 July. It would have been received, therefore, after the commission had sent its report to the Archbishop. Dr Lennon's letter enumerates and comments on several possible natural explanations: collusion, phosphorescent paint, magic lantern, illusion, hallucination. One of them, the magic lantern theory, he has investigated for himself, and considers it 'morally speaking, impossible'. In regard to the other theories he makes some comment, and mentions circumstances which seem to favour one or other of the possibilities, and which, he says, should be taken into consideration by the commission. He concludes that these other possibilities have not been proved to be inadmissible.

At the beginning of his letter Dr Lennon warns that his opinion 'was founded entirely on the evidence produced on the occasion of his visit'. During his visit he personally examined four witnesses. He does not say whether he read the depositions or not, but some of his remarks seem to show that he was unaware of some evidence contained in them. The general impression gathered from his letter is that he was not taking it upon himself to pronounce a judgement on any of the natural possibilities except one. He urges careful consideration of the others, but does not profess to have made any detailed investigation of them. He puts the onus of such investigation on the commission.

It was to be expected that the priests on the commission would themselves be aware of the various possible explanations. That they were so aware is shown in the first place by the many seemingly insignificant details elicited from the witnesses. Many of those details are of special importance in relation to the various theories that required consideration. It is scarcely possible that they would have been sought after except by a well-informed inquirer. Second, in the fourth chapter of his booklet, which was published before Dr Lennon's letter was written, MacPhilpin discusses several possible explanations: conspiracy, delusion, reflected light, a magic lantern, the effect of phosphorus, electric or magnetic currents. His reasoning on these matters is, on the whole, sound, and displays a knowledge uncommon for a layman. It would not be unreasonable to assume that in this he was echoing to some extent the deliberations of the commission, especially as his uncle, Canon Bourke, was a member of the commission, and because uncle and nephew had been in close cooperation in their work for the newspaper. So, available evidence goes to show that the commission was in possession of expert information.

The depositions are the only part of the commission's work which has survived. From them we can gather that the commission approached their task with care and in a scientific manner. There are four witnesses to whom the commission gave special attention, and from whom they were at pains to get accurate, detailed and decisive information. These are Patrick Hill, Mary McLoughlin, Mary Beirne and Mrs Bridget Trench. The depositions of the others are of varying degrees of value. One notes in the depositions of Dominick Beirne, Jr, that he refers to the figures 'that have already been described'. Inserted in the deposition of Patrick Beirne we find: 'Young Beirne then told what he saw regarding the vision, just as it has been described already by several persons who were present.' In the *Weekly News* version, Mrs Margaret Beirne states that 'the image of St Joseph appeared as just described by the others who have given testimony', and immediately after these words we have inserted in brackets the note: 'witness did not hear the testimony, but she repeated it, and it coincides with all that already given.' From these observations it is clear that the reporter did not record everything that was said by the witnesses. Where he saw there was a repetition he summarised. However, the depositions as a whole show that the investigation was thorough and enlightened.

The commission examined fifteen witnesses, fourteen who saw the apparition at the church gable, and one who saw the light over the church from half a mile away. It is certain that more than fourteen people witnessed the scene at the church gable. Mrs O'Connell (nee Mary Beirne) in statements made in 1932 and 1936 mentioned three other women – Peggy Mullee, Margaret Mannion and Mrs Tom Curry, who saw the apparition but were not examined by the commission. Evidence was given before the

1936 Commission that a man named James Coyne also saw the apparition, and that he had gone to England in October when the commission was taking the statements. There is a local tradition that the very first person to see the strange sight at the church gable was a Mrs Carty, who had passed by on the road some time before seven o'clock. When she saw the figures, she thought, as others who came after her thought, that they were statues. Her thoughts did not turn to the supernatural. Rather did she forecast that there would probably be another parish collection to pay for this latest consignment of statues. She went her way and thought no more of the matter until next day, when she heard the talk about the apparition that was seen at the church the evening before. Why the commission did not examine all the witnesses we do not know. It may be that more than one of them had gone to England in the meantime, as there was much emigration from the locality in that year. It is possible, too, that after examining fifteen witnesses the commission considered they had sufficient evidence.

The report submitted by the commission to the Archbishop is published by John MacPhilpin in the following manner: 'His Grace the Archbishop of Tuam ordered the depositions of the several witnesses to be taken by a commission of learned priests and dignitaries deputed for that purpose, and they have reported officially that the testimony of all, taken as a whole, is trustworthy and satisfactory.'[3] There is no official record of the report, but MacPhilpin's statement, for reasons already given, can be accepted as reliable. What assent is to be given to this verdict? It is not, of course, an authoritative decision, but the commission was competent to submit its findings; its members were well informed on the nature of apparitions and their counterfeits; they personally examined the witnesses, and being parish priests in the district of Knock and the surrounding area, they were in a position to know and judge the character of the witnesses who came before them; they considered the facts of the case and possible explanations. Therefore their report can be accepted as expert opinion.

What is the exact import of the commission's report? The

witnesses claimed to have seen a heavenly apparition. The commission declared their evidence to be trustworthy and satisfactory. From this one may conclude that the claim appeared well founded, and that the evidence could be believed. It may be objected that an obstacle to unhesitating assent to this opinion arises from the lack of records of the deliberations of the commission and of the processes of reasoning by which they arrived at their conclusion. Prescinding from the question as to whether the objection is reasonably grounded or not one may concede that uncertainty concerning a link in the chain of evidence causes uncertainty concerning the conclusion. In order, therefore, to put the story of Knock on a firm basis it is necessary to start with what is certain.

To sum up the foregoing pages we can be reasonably certain the three deputed priests examined fifteen witnesses; that each witness told his or her story of the apparition; that the commission formulated a statement embodying the evidence of each witness; that even if the commission did nothing other than examine the witnesses and record the evidence, they have left to posterity sufficient material from which to draw conclusions based on scientific principles; even though the original documents are lost, we can be reasonably certain that the published versions of the statements of the witnesses are authentic copies.[4]

In the next chapter it is proposed to apply the principles of a methodic inquiry to the statements for the purpose of ascertaining what conclusions can be drawn from them. Use will be made of evidence given by witnesses after 1879 and in particular of evidence taken by the commission which was set up in 1936 by Most Rev. Dr Gilmartin, Archbishop of Tuam. The judges in this commission were: Rt Rev. Monsignor E.A. D'Alton, Dean of the Chapter, PP, V.G., Ballinrobe; Very Rev. Stephen Canon Walsh, PP, VF, Dunmore; Very Rev. Denis Canon Ryder, PP, Ballindine; Rev. John Killeen, Adm., Tuam, was Promoter Fidei; and Rev. James S. Fergus, Archbishop's Secretary, was Secretary of the commission. The evidence taken was given under oath. There were fifteen sessions. The first session was held on 24 August 1936, and the last on 14 April 1939. The commission examined two surviving eyewitnesses of the apparition, Mrs O'Connell (nee Mary Beirne) and Patrick Beirne. Mrs O'Connell was eighty-six years old at the time. The commission visited her home, and she gave her evidence from her sick bed. She died some weeks later. Patrick Beirne was examined in the sacristy of Knock church.

John Curry, another surviving eyewitness – he was six years old at the time of the apparition – was living in New York in 1936. A request was sent by the commission through the Archbishop of Tuam to Cardinal Hayes, Archbishop of New York, asking that John Curry be officially examined on the 1879 apparition. A special tribunal was set up by the Archbishop of New York, before which John Curry was examined under oath. A copy of the Acts of the New York tribunal was sent to the Archbishop of Tuam and is incorporated into the Acts of the Tuam Commission.

Twelve residents of Knock who had heard the story of the apparition from eyewitnesses were questioned on what they heard, and on the reliability of the eyewitnesses. Four priests who had ministered at Knock at different times since 1895 were questioned concerning the reliability of the eyewitnesses, the nature of the pilgrimages and the devotion of the pilgrims. Mr William Coyne, District Justice, was questioned concerning the sources consulted for his book, *Knock Shrine.* Dr George Maguire, Secretary of the Medical Bureau at Knock, gave evidence concerning the Bureau itself and cures which it had examined. Eight cases of reported cures were examined by the commission, Dr Maguire being the official Medical Assessor.

The commission in its inquiry conducted what is technically called a *processus informativus.* Its purpose was to take evidence. It was not entrusted with the task of making a decision on the origin of the apparition, but in submitting their report the Judges stated that all the witnesses examined by them were judged to be 'upright and trustworthy'.

8.

An Inquiry

In their depositions the witnesses claim to have seen an apparition. There are several possible explanations for the phenomenon they report. It may have been due to supernatural agency, or it may have been due to natural causes. If it is possible to explain the occurrence by a natural cause, then supernatural agency may not be postulated. The following are natural causes that must be examined as possible explanations of the apparition at Knock:

I.   Fabrication by the witnesses.
II. Deception by some person or persons unknown.
III. Imagination.

We shall examine each of these in turn.

I. Fabrication
Did the witnesses invent the story and deliberately publish falsehood?

In answer to this question we have the following considerations:
(a) The witnesses were simple, hardworking, good-living people. They had a deep-rooted respect for religion. They were not the type to spread a deliberate falsehood about Our Lady and the Saints.
(b) The witnesses were fifteen in number of different ages and sexes and condition. All told the same story except for minor

divergencies. They all continued to tell the same story up to the time of death. None of them retracted. In 1936 the three surviving witnesses confirmed on oath their testimony of 1879, making corrections that did not affect the substance of the story. That fifteen Catholic people of such varied conditions and outlook should conspire to invent a story about Our Lady and the Saints, and preserve such uniformity in their evidence, and continue to tell the same story till their deaths, is morally impossible. The only conclusion that can be drawn from such uniform and tenacious adherence to a story by diverse characters is that they were telling what they believed to be true.

(c) People who knew the witnesses testified that they were reliable and could be believed.

(i) The 1879 Commission 'reported officially that the testimony of all, taken as a whole, is trustworthy and satisfactory'.[1] Even though one may not be satisfied for want of complete records to accept that the commission proved the divine origin of the apparition, nevertheless, their opinion on the truthfulness of the witnesses is evidence that must be taken as expert and cannot be disregarded. The three priests had personally examined the witnesses and questioned them on their story; they were parish priests in the locality, and they understood the mentality of the people.

(ii) Twelve residents of Knock who knew the witnesses testified under oath before the 1936 Commission that the witnesses they knew were reliable and would not have made up the story; that the people of Knock believed in the apparition, even though some critics from outside doubted it.

(iii) Four priests who had ministered at Knock at different times from 1895 to 1936, one or two of whom did not show enthusiasm for the apparition, testified that the witnesses they knew were truthful, and that they were not capable of fabricating the story. One of the priests had doubts about the reliability of one of the witnesses (not any of the important witnesses), but he gave no evidence to prove untruthfulness in the witness in question.

(d) Fr Thurston, who did much scientific research on apparitions, while not satisfied that the divine origin of the Knock apparition was established from the evidence available to him at the time of writing, nevertheless, says this of the witnesses: 'I find it very hard to believe that these people, simple folk of all ages – one of them, Bridget Trench, was seventy-five, and Patrick Walsh, sixty-five – were deliberately lying, when they stated that they stood or knelt for an hour or more looking at these motionless figures and the illuminated wall of the church in the pouring rain.

The fact that it was a wet night seems to me to add enormously to the difficulty of supposing that the manifestation was in any way got up with any fraudulent purpose.'[2]

(e) Mrs O'Connell (nee Mary Beirne) came to be regarded as the most important witness of the apparition. She was the first to consider the sight a heavenly manifestation; she summoned many of the other witnesses; she was in the group that was last to leave the scene; she was known generally for her intelligence, her deep faith, her solid piety. During her long life she was interviewed by many inquirers. She received them all with courtesy, and answered their questions with simplicity. The priests and lay people who gave evidence before the 1936 Commission had no hesitation in declaring her to be truthful and reliable.

In 1880 the *Weekly News* published a reporter's interview with Mary Beirne, the substance of which is given in the following extract:[3]

'I understand, Miss Beirne,' I said, 'that you saw an extraordinary appearance here at the chapel of Knock.'

'Yes, Sir, I did.'

'When did you see it?'

'On the 21 August.'

'At what hour?'

'About eight o'clock in the evening.'

'There was daylight at the time?'

'There was; good light.'

'Where were you?'

'I was going from the house to the chapel.'

'Were you alone?'

'No; Mary McLoughlin, Fr Cavanagh's housekeeper, was with me.'

'Why were you going to the chapel at eight o'clock in the evening?'

'I was going to lock it up.'[4]

'Well?'

'When we got to the wall by the schoolhouse, I looked up to the chapel, and I saw the three statues.'

'Did the figures look like statues?'

'Yes; they looked so like statues that I thought Fr Cavanagh was after sending for them, and I wondered he never told us about them.'

'What size were they?'

'About the same size as living people.'

'And what colour?'

'White.'

'Now describe the figure that appeared to be next the road.'

'St Joseph was at the end of the gable. There was a stoop in him, and he was facing towards the Blessed Virgin. I remarked his venerable grey hair and whiskers. His side face turned to us.'

'What was the next figure?'

'The Blessed Virgin Mary. Her full face was turned out. Her two hands were raised up this way. [The posture was exactly that illustrated by Dominick Beirne.] Her eyes were raised up in the form of praying.'

'Was every part of the figure the same colour as all the rest of it?'

'No; she wore a beautiful crown; it looked like gold; and the face appeared to be a yellower white than the body of the cloak.'

'How was the figure robed?'

'There was one large cloak pinned to the neck, and falling loose over the arms, and there was another garment inside; it was tighter to the figure, and there was something like "puffing" up the front of it.'

'Did you see the feet?'

'No; I couldn't see them; I think the robe covered them.'

'What was the third figure?'

'St John. He was to the left of the Blessed Virgin. He appeared wearing a mitre and a long robe. He was partly turned away from the other figures, facing a plain altar, like marble, with a lamb on the altar, and a cross on the lamb's shoulder. There was a large book, like a missal, open on the left hand, and his right hand was raised up, with the two fingers next us bent.'

In 1932 she made a statement before a board of priests (consisting of Canon Grealy, PP, Knock; Canon McHugh, PP, Claremorris; Fr Martin Flynn, CC, Ballyhaunis; Fr T.A. Jennings, St Jarlath's College, Tuam). The following is the full statement:

'I was twenty-eight years old at the time of the Apparition. It took place on 21 August 1879. I was in my house when Mary McLoughlin came in to visit us. I accompanied her home on her return. When about a hundred yards from the church, we noticed what appeared to be statues at the church gable. I asked my friend, "When did the Archdeacon put the statues at the gable?" She replied, "He never got them, whoever put them there". On approaching nearer to the gable we noticed the figures were surrounded by an extraordinary light. We now realised that there was no question of statues, but of something supernatural. There were three figures. In the centre was the Blessed Virgin clothed in a long cloak closed at the neck and wearing a white crown on her head. St Joseph was on one side, and in a position facing the Blessed Virgin. On the other side was St John the Evangelist, whose identity was disclosed by the resemblance between a statue of St John and this figure. In his left hand he held a book; his right hand was somewhat raised with the index and middle fingers pointing upwards. On his head was a mitre. The figure of St Joseph appeared more life-like, having more colour in the face than the other figures. It was raining at the time, but no rain fell on the figures. The figures stood about one foot from the ground and on a level with the long grass at the gable. The figures gave no indication of life, but although they seemed to stand out from the wall, receded when approached. On seeing this vision I returned home and told the other members of my family of what I had seen. They followed me to the scene. Meanwhile Mary McLoughlin, housekeeper to Archdeacon Cavanagh, went to the parochial house to acquaint the parish priest of the occurrence. He, however, did not visit the scene, believing, as he told his housekeeper, that it was a reflection from a stained-glass window erected some time before. The following people were present – amongst members of my own family were my mother, my sister Margaret, my brother Dominick and Catherine Murray. In addition to these there were present Mary McLoughlin [already mentioned], Mrs Carney, Peggy Mullee, Margaret Mannion, Mrs Tom Curry, John Durkan, Pat Hill, Dominick Beirne and Pat Beirne. Mrs Carney [nee Trench] approached the wall to touch the figures, but told us there was nothing substantial there, exclaiming, "Níl tada annseo".

'I remained there until 9.45 p.m. and then returned home. After about a quarter of an hour I returned to the church accompanied by my brother Dominick Beirne. By this time there was no trace of the Apparition.'

This statement was not under oath.

It will be observed that she omits to mention here the altar, the lamb and the cross. She also omits mention of the sudden departure to Mrs Campbell's home. She describes Our Lady's crown as white. It had been described before this as a gold colour. Omissions and discrepancies of this kind are due to mistakes somewhere, but do not discredit the evidence.

In 1935 an interview given to Liam Ua Cahdain (William Coyne) was published in his book, *Knock Shrine*. The following is the portion of the interview relevant to the present context:[5]

'She tells us that the Blessed Virgin wore all white, without a trace of blue anywhere; and she wore no rings and as far as she could see there was no Rosary beads in her hands, which were raised in prayer. "I remember it all so well," she goes on, "as if it happened today … Our house was then on the east side of the church and adjoining the grounds, and on that night the priest's housekeeper had called to welcome home the people who had just returned from the seaside at Lecanvey … I was leaving her home and on the way we passed the south gable of the church when I called attention to the vision." "But," she added sadly, "we were lost that the priest did not come to see it." She was convinced that the favour of the vision vouchsafed Knock on account of the holiness of the Archdeacon. He had a very deep devotion to the Holy Souls, and he had just then completed one hundred Masses for them. "The light about the figures was not like any light I ever saw but more like the soft silvery light of the moon. And I also remember well Archbishop Murphy [of Tasmania], who came on a visit of thanksgiving. One day at the gable wall he addressed those of us gathered there, and told us to pray with great confidence that it was not the statue but Our Lady herself that had come there and that he himself was cured through her intercession." She went on to tell how two commissioners took her evidence in the school house, and a fortnight later twenty more priests arrived, some of whose names she remembered distinctly, and carried out elaborate tests with magic lantern slides. "They wanted to make out," she said, "that the pictures were like the ones we saw, but they were no more like them and no one could make them like the apparitions.""

The commission in fact sat in the sacristy, not in the school, and there were three commissioners, not two. She later corrected the latter statement.

On 27 January 1936, she made a sworn statement before a Commissioner for Oaths and Canon Grealy: in this statement she describes the scene: Our Lady, St Joseph, St John, the altar and lamb. At the end of the statement she adds: 'I am quite clear about everything I have said, and I make this statement knowing I am going before my God.'

On 27 August 1936, she was visited by the members of the 1936 Commission. She was eighty-six years old at the time, and was confined to bed, expecting death in a short time. The deposition she made before the 1879 Commission, as published by MacPhilpin, was read to her by Canon Walsh, and she was asked if she confirmed it. She replied as follows: 'There was an uncut meadow at the gable, and they were standing on the top of the grass. They were not pressing down the grass. We knew they were not statues.

'About the hands I would not like to swear to that. I am thinking for a long time about the position of the hands, and it seems to me that the hands were down like that, by her side. But I am not so sure about that.

'When we went near the wall, the figures seemed to go back to the wall, as if painted on it. Then when we came back from the wall, they seemed to stand out and come forward.

'About St Joseph, I don't know about the grey hair. But he looked old, and his colour not so white as the Blessed Virgin. Anyone could know St Joseph. I don't remember now about the book in St John's hand, or about the way he held his fingers, or that his hand was stretched towards the Blessed

Virgin. I remember him clothed in a cloak falling down in folds like a Bishop.

'I don't remember about seeing the lamb, but the others did. I didn't see the stars, but the others did.

'We never spoke a word the fifteen of us during the time we were looking at the apparition – an hour and a quarter like as if we were statues.

'Subject to the above alterations I confirm the deposition read to me.'

She was asked if she saw the *Weekly News* interview, and she said, 'Yes'. When asked if it was correct she replied: 'It was very near. I won't swear to what it said about the cross.' She was asked if she confirmed the interview in Liam Ua Cadhain's book, and she said 'Yes', but she made a correction concerning the 1879 Commission. She was examined before three commissioners, not two. She gave the additional information that Archdeacon Cavanagh had completed one hundred Masses for the Holy Souls the very morning of the apparition.

The commission did not question her on the 1932 statement.

Asked if she confirmed the affidavit sworn before the Commissioner for Oaths, she replied: 'I do confirm it, but I don't remember that I said anything about the book or the lamb. I might have said it, but I don't remember.'

The judges of the 1936 Commission stated in their report that 'Mary O'Connell left a most favourable impression' on their minds.

It is perhaps needless to draw attention to the naturalness, simple charm and conviction of the above evidence given by a devout Irish country woman, as she lay on her death bed, in her eighty-sixth year. There is evident in her story a tenderness of conscience, and a keen awareness of the sacredness of her oath, which causes her to distinguish very carefully between the information of which she feels sure, and that of which she is not certain. This enhances the reliability of her evidence. It is not to be wondered at, if at her age and in her sickness, her memory should fail in regard to details of an event that took place fifty-seven years previously – detail such as the position of Our Lady's hands or the book in St John's hand. Her first statements on these points may safely be taken as correct. She seems quite definite she did not see the stars. She says she does not remember seeing the lamb. The lamb is mentioned in her affidavit of the 27 January. Of that affidavit she says: 'I don't remember that I said anything about the book or lamb. I might have said it, but I don't remember.' Because of her old age, and her sickness, her memory failed her on this point.

Her last statement is not that she did not see the lamb, but, 'I don't remember seeing the lamb'. One thing is clear from her evidence – she is obviously telling what she considers to be the truth in giving the information of which she is certain, and her evidence of 1879 is confirmed without substantial change. Furthermore, her deliberation in making her statements shows that she was not following a formula learned by rote, but that she was speaking from direct memory of experience.

(f) Patrick Beirne was sixteen years old at the time of the apparition. If one is to judge by the amount of his evidence recorded by the 1879 Commission, he was not considered by them to be one of the more important witnesses. His evidence appears to be treated merely as corroborative.

He made the following statement before the board of priests in 1932: 'I saw three figures on the gable surrounded by wonderful light. They appeared to be something like shadows or reflections cast on a wall on a moonlight night. I approached nearer the gable and passed my hand along the wall to find there was no material substance there. The figures were towards the left hand side of the gable. The figures were those of the Blessed Virgin in the central position; to the right of the Blessed Virgin was St Joseph, and to the left was a figure suggested by a bystander to represent St John the Evangelist. To the right of the group, and at a higher level, was a figure of a lamb in a reclining position and facing the figures. I spent between twenty minutes and a half an hour there when I returned home.'

In January 1936 he made a sworn statement before a Commissioner for Oaths. The statement is in the diocesan archives and is as follows:

'I, Patrick Beirne, of Knock in the County of Mayo, aged seventy-one years and upwards, make oath and say: I remember the evening of 21 August 1879. My attention was called by another man named Dominick Beirne to a vision consisting of three figures, the Blessed Virgin, St Joseph and St John. It was then about nine o'clock. I was informed when I came on the scene that the vision was there since about a quarter to eight o'clock. The figure of the Blessed Virgin was in the centre; St Joseph was in the right; he was turned sideways and facing the Blessed Virgin. St John was on the Blessed Virgin's left. He had a book in his hand. The Blessed Virgin had a very brilliant crown on her head. She wore a brilliant white cloak. To the left of St John was a lamb lying on his side on the altar. The whole gable was lit up with a brilliant light. There was a heavy drizzle of rain. The rain did not appear to fall on the figures or on the light. There were about fourteen or fifteen people there watching the vision with me; amongst them was Mrs Mary O'Connell, who is still living in Knock; she was then Mary Beirne. I remained there about an hour and I then went home.'

In August 1936 he was examined by the 1936 Commission. The following are some of the questions put to Patrick Beirne by the commission and the answers given by him:

'Do you confirm the deposition as it was published by John MacPhilpin in 1880?'

'I confirm that deposition which I have now read, all except the statement, "I remained only ten minutes and then went away". This statement is incorrect. I came at nine o'clock and I remained until twenty past ten.'

'Do you confirm the affidavit of 27 January 1936 sworn before William Paul Mongey, Commissioner for Oaths?'

'I have just now read this affidavit and I confirm what is in it. There is nothing in it that needs amending except that I would say that the lamb was standing rather than lying on its side.'

'Was the brightness you saw pale like the moonlight or like sunlight?'

'The whole gable was as bright as snow. I could not describe to you what kind the light was, but that it was there and that it was brilliant. It must be some supernatural light.'

'Were the figures very clear and distinct?'

'They were as clear and distinct as you could see any human being here.'

Although Patrick Beirne was not considered one of the more important witnesses by the 1879 Commission, he was given much prominence at the end of his life, because he was the last witness to die. People who knew him said he was always 'a little bit odd'. One of the priests stated before the 1936 Commission that he would not consider him a reliable witness, and mentioned something concerning him which was much talked of in the locality, but the evidence the priest gives does not imply untruthfulness. If Patrick Beirne failed to fulfil his religious duties for some time, it was a lamentable lapse, but it did not prove that he did not see the apparition. The twelve witnesses who gave evidence before the 1936 Commission all testified that they had no reason to doubt his truthfulness. All through his life Patrick Beirne affirmed he saw the apparition. He did not retract anything before death. The judges of the 1936 Commission state in their report:

'Patrick Beirne is of a slightly difficult disposition and, as it seemed to us, he considers himself as a person of some importance, but nevertheless he is judged by us to be upright and truthful.'

If we are to take an objective view of the evidence, it does not seem possible to deny that Patrick Beirne saw the apparition. It is not easy to doubt his truthfulness. One may, however, have doubts about the accuracy of his memory. He is describing what happened fifty-seven years before the time of speaking. In his several statements he makes changes in matters of detail. In his last statement he shows a definite self-assurance in regard to details – an assurance which, in view of his emendations, one may feel is not entirely well grounded. In this he makes a striking contrast with Mrs O'Connell, who is hesitant about details, and who speaks with an obvious straining for accuracy. Furthermore the fact that he considered himself 'a person of some importance' would indicate that he might in later life unconsciously augment what he actually saw with embellishments of his own. The final assessment of Patrick Beirne's evidence would seem to be that it has corroborative value, but is not necessary for probative purposes.

(g) John Curry was examined by the New York tribunal on 6 July 1937. At that time he was living in one of the homes of the Little Sisters of the Poor in New York. Both the Mother Superior and the Chaplain of the Home testified that they found him very truthful and of good character. He served Mass very devoutly every morning and received Holy Communion almost daily. As he was only six years old at the time of the apparition, it can scarcely be expected that he would be clear on everything that he saw. On some things he was confused. The following are some questions and answers taken from the report:

'Describe what you saw at the church gable as well as you can recall.'

'I seen the Blessed Virgin, St Joseph and St John the Evangelist on the gable of the church. St Joseph was on the right hand side of the Blessed Virgin, and St John was on the left hand, as I recall. There was a kind of an altar, plain with no ornaments on it, at the back of the vision. There was a lamb there, but I could not see whether the lamb was on the altar or under St Joseph's arm, because St Joseph's arm was raised [witness made a gesture with his left arm to show the position of St Joseph's arm, which witness raised and crooked at a level just below the shoulder]. The lamb was between the Blessed Virgin and St Joseph. St John the Evangelist had a Gospel book in his left hand and his right hand raised [witness made a gesture describing the right hand raised and open with finger-tips about on eye level with palm facing outward]. The Blessed Virgin was all dressed in white; she wore a crown on her head and had her hands folded before her in prayer. Our Lady's face was just like you would see on a statue. That is, as far as I can recall.

'St Joseph had whiskers, but I don't think he wore a hat. I can remember St John good, but I don't remember St Joseph so well. St John was dressed in white like a priest or bishop and he had a book in his hand. It wasn't a Mass book, I don't think, because it was too small, but a Gospel book. I think you would call it. On his head he wore what I think you call a mitre, a little round hat.'

'Did the figures appear to be alive?'

'Yes, it appeared to me that they were alive, but they did not speak. One of the women there, Bridget Trench, kissed the Blessed Virgin's feet and tried to put her arms around the feet but there was nothing there but just the picture. I saw her do that. The figures were life-size, and I will remember them till I go to my grave.'

'Did the figures move?'

'I did not see the figures move, but there seemed to be two angels – I didn't know they were angels until I was told – moving back and forth. I asked Pat Hill and he told me they were angels.'

'Was there anything unusual about the light?'

'No, except that it seemed to come from the angels moving back and forth.'

'Have you read the depositions of the eyewitnesses as they were published at Tuam in 1880 by John MacPhilpin, and as they were quoted in the recently published book, *Knock Shrine*, by Mr W.D. Coyne, D.J.?'

'I never read any book by Mr Coyne in this country, but I read all about the apparition in the old country, when I was a boy going to school. Just before I came into this hearing I was given a book, and the only part of it I read was the statements by Patrick Hill and Catherine Murray.'

'Were the answers you gave independent of what you read here and elsewhere?'

'What I gave here was out of my own head and not out of any book.'

'Do you confirm what is said by these witnesses about yourself, and do you consider that the depositions of the other eyewitnesses, as quoted, are a true description of what you saw yourself?'

'I confirm what is said about myself as the truth, and the depositions, as far as I have read, of the other witnesses are the truth.'

After he had given his evidence he was shown a picture of the apparition and was asked if it represented what he saw on 21 August 1879. He replied: 'That is the picture all right, but I am under the impression that the lamb was on St Joseph's side, but I am not sure of that. He might have been on St John's side. I can't swear to that.'

(h) Dr Lennon in his letter to Archdeacon Cavanagh refers to the witnesses examined by him and says: 'The witnesses examined were Miss Beirne and her brother – both of full age, and highly intelligent; a woman aged seventy-four years; and subsequently a boy, named Hill, whose statement, however, I regard as of little or no value.' Dr Lennon gives no reason for his unwillingness to accept Patrick Hill's statement. Presumably, it was because he was only thirteen years old. It is significant that he mentions the ages of the other three, and later in his letter, he quotes an authority who suspects apparitions seen by the young.

Psychologists' distrust of young people's apparitions is a presumption which yields to contrary proof. The following considerations favour the reliability of Patrick Hill's story of the apparition.

- The commission regarded his statement as trustworthy and satisfactory. His home was in Claremorris in the same street as the parish priest's residence. Canon Bourke, therefore, as parish priest of Claremorris was in a favourable position to evaluate the boy's testimony. Of all the statements taken by the commission the longest and most detailed was that given by Patrick Hill. This shows in a special way that the commission regarded him as reliable. MacPhilpin, in giving the depositions of the witnesses, places Patrick Hill's statement first with the preface: 'In presenting the testimony of the different witnesses … the first place is rightly due to the evidence of Patrick Hill, of Claremorris, a young, frank and intelligent boy of about thirteen years of age. His account of the apparition is the fullest and most satisfactory.'[6]

- Further evidence of the regard which Canon Bourke had for the testimony of Patrick Hill is provided by the fact that when inquirers – including the representatives of the *Weekly News* and *Daily Telegraph* – called on Canon Bourke for information on Knock, he referred them to Patrick Hill.

- The report of the two newspapers are of value as offering an opportunity for comparing three accounts given by him on three different occasions. The *Weekly News* representative visited Canon Bourke in Claremorris and wrote as follows:[7]

'His Reverence kindly gave me every facility in his power for learning as much as could be known of the facts of the case. One of the witnesses – a little boy named Patrick Hill –

lives in Claremorris, and Canon Bourke sent a messenger for him, that I might myself interrogate him on the subject.

'Patrick Hill is a frank, intelligent little boy of about thirteen years. He answers the questions put to him readily and with animation. The following is the chief portion of the conversation which passed between him and me:

"Well, Pat, you live in Claremorris, don't you?"

"Yes, sir."

"How came you to see the vision?"

"My aunt lives at Knock, sir, and I go there sometimes; on this night a man ran into my aunt's house and called us to come up to the chapel to see a miraculous sight that was there. The man's name was Dominick Beirne."

"Then you went out; did anyone else go with you?"

"Yes, sir, another man of the same name, Dominick Beirne, John Durkan, a servant boy, and a little boy named John Curry, about six years old."

"Were there any persons there before you?"

"Oh, yes, sir, there were people coming and going."

"Well, Pat, what did you see?"

'Here the little boy proceeded to describe the vision. He said he and the other persons who were with him saw a large space of soft white light on the gable of the church, the rest of the gable being quite dark at the time. In the midst of this light, which was not exactly in the centre, but towards the left hand side of the gable [as he stood facing it] he saw three figures; to his left, in a bending attitude, with hands clasped, was a figure of St Joseph; in the middle a figure of the Virgin, her eyes raised, her hands raised to about the level of her shoulders, and their palms turned outwards; to his [the witness's] right a figure of a bishop, which the people said was St John, holding in his left hand an open book, which he appeared to be reading, his right hand elevated, the thumb placed on the third and fourth fingers, the first and second standing erect. Farther on to his [the witness's] right appeared an altar with a lamb on it as represented in Catholic pictures, and a cross standing in the altar. All about the group was the twinkling of flashing lights, like stars; they were not steady; they seemed as if they used to come nearer and then retire again, or to go in and out through the gable.

"Was the night dark at the time, Pat?"

"Yes, sir, and it was raining very hard; we were all getting wet, but we did not mind it."

"Did there appear to be any light in the clouds overhead, or back of you anywhere?"

"No, sir, not a bit."

"Where were you standing at the time?"

"Part of the time I and some of the others stood behind the low little wall that bounds the chapel field; we rested our elbows on it and looked at the visions, and the little boy that was with me [Curry] asked me to lift him up to see the beautiful things that were in the gable of the church. Part of the time we were in the field, and quite near to the gable."

"Did the figures appear quite distinct and round?"

"They did, sir."

"Could you have touched them?"

"Yes, sir; and an old woman that was there tried to put her hands round the Virgin's feet."

"Did you see the Virgin's feet?"

'Yes, sir, from the ankles down. She wore a white dress that reached to her ankles."

"How high from the ground were the feet of the figures?"

"About a foot and a half."

"How long did you remain there?"

"More than an hour. People were coming and going all the time. They all saw the vision."

"What were you talking about while you were there?"

"About nothing only what we saw."

"Did you say your prayers?"

"Oh, yes, sir; all the people went on their knees and were saying the Rosary and their prayers.'"

The *Daily Telegraph* has the following:

'Canon Bourke, having acted on a commission appointed by the Archbishop of Tuam to take the evidence of those who asserted that they had seen the apparitions, was well able to put me in the way of ascertaining particulars for myself, and within an hour of my introduction to him, I was face to face with one of the persons who deposed to the August vision. This was a boy of about fourteen years of age, named Patrick Hill – a bright, intelligent little fellow, who told his tale clearly and simply. I shall put Hill's statement in the first person, without pledging myself, however, to literal exactness, and premising that the narrative was not continuous, but frequently interrupted by questions needless to repeat here: "I sometimes go out to the bog for turf, and did so on the day of the August apparition, taking my little brother with me. When night came on, I went into the house of a relative, not far from Knock chapel. It was raining hard and very dark. While there someone [naming him] ran in and said: Oh come up to the chapel, and see the Blessed Virgin against the wall! We all ran up, and saw the end of the chapel covered with light; at first we stood against the wall of the yard, but presently we got over and went up close to the gable. Then we saw the Blessed Virgin standing like a statue so [lifting his hands and eyes]; on her right was St Joseph, bending towards her, and on her left St John, dressed like a bishop, his left hand holding a book, his right raised, with two fingers pointing upwards. Above, and to the left of St John, was an altar with a lamb on it, round which moved what seemed to be the wings of angels, whose heads and bodies I could not see."'[8]

It will be seen that the three accounts are in agreement.

- Mrs O'Connell in her sworn affidavit of 1936 mentioned Patrick Hill as one of those present at the apparition.
- In 1937, John Curry confirmed before the New York tribunal what was said of him in Patrick Hill's deposition, and also stated the following:

'The boy that was with me, Pat Hill – I could not see at first, there was a wall around the church along by the road – and Pat Hill lifted me up on the wall … I did not know what to do. Pat Hill told me what it was and explained it.'

- Nearly all of Patrick Hill's deposition is confirmed by the depositions of the other witnesses.
- Patrick Hill was in a better position for observing details than the others. He went closer to the apparition than the group of adults. He stood right beside the figures. Being young, curious and observant, he saw things others did not see. He saw the rose on Our Lady's forehead, and noticed the parts of her eyes; he saw angels fluttering around the head of the lamb, and observed the lettering of the book in St John's hand. His statements on the essentials and most of the details are borne out by the other witnesses. The information that is given by himself alone can be relied on because of the concurrence of the mass of his evidence with that of the others, because of his advantageous position for special observation, and because of the belief of the commission in his general reliability.
- There is no evidence that he ever retracted any of his testimony. He died in Boston, USA, in 1927.

(i) What is considered an unfavourable circumstance is that some of the witnesses were said to have derived pecuniary gain from the apparition. There is no evidence whatever that the witnesses had any motive for gain when they told the news of the apparition. If some material benefits did accrue to a few of the witnesses, this does not imply untruthfulness. Furthermore the criticism does not apply to those witnesses who derived no gain from the story.

(j) No criticism directed against any of the witnesses has ever proved untruthfulness in the story of the apparition.

The conclusion, therefore, is that the volume of evidence proving the truthfulness of the witnesses is so overwhelming that fabrication cannot be admitted as an explanation of the apparition.

II. Deception by Some Person or Persons Unknown

Such deception could have been wrought in one or other of two ways:

   (a) By the painting of images on the wall or on a canvas with a phosphorescent substance.

   (b) By the projection of images on the wall with a specially constructed camera (magic lantern).

(a) *Phosphorescent Painting*

In her 1936 evidence, Mrs O'Connell said that, when they went near the wall, the figures seemed to go back to the wall 'as if painted on it'. It is known that phosphorescent paint is luminous in the dark and can be used to make a brilliant picture. Could the Knock apparition have been produced by painting the wall with phosphorescent paint? The following considerations supply an answer:

(i) Painting the figures on the wall would have required time and labour, and could not have been done without the aid of scaffolding. Such activity could not have been carried on at the church gable unknown to the people of the locality.

(ii) Such a painting would have required a person skilled in the use of phosphorus and at the same time an artist of ability and originality. No such person was heard of in the neighbourhood.

(iii) Mrs O'Connell was asked at the 1936 hearing if they had seen any fresh paint or wash on the gable of the church the evening of the apparition or during the days afterwards, and her reply was: 'We did not, although we came back that night after the apparition had gone, and several times within the next few days.'

A possibility that might appear more likely is that a canvas painted with phosphorescent paint was hung on the wall. The following points are offered against this suggestion. They are also relevant to the possibility of paint on the wall itself.

(i) The first sight that Mary Beirne and Mary McLoughlin got of the figures was from a side view about three hundred yards off. The figures appeared to them from that angle and distance as statues. That could not have happened if the figures were mere painting.

(ii) Phosphorescent paint is not luminous in the day time. The apparition was seen while it was still day from three hundred yards off.

(iii) Phosphorescent paint could not be seen half a mile away even at night time. Patrick Walsh saw an extraordinary bright light over the church from his land. His position was not south of the gable, but to the east. Consequently, he had only a side view of the gable. Phosphorus could not have cast such an extraordinary light into the sky.

(iv) Phosphorus is fitful and continually fluctuating, and does not present static outlines nor minutely defined features. The images seen by the witnesses were settled, presenting an accurately defined outline. 'They were full and round as if they had body and life.' Patrick Hill saw the parts of Our Lady's eyes and the writing in the book in St John's hand. This would have been impossible with phosphorus.

(v) Rain and a wet surface would have so considerably lessened the effect of phosphorus that it could not be mistaken for the apparition.

(vi) Phosphorus does not explain the stoppage of rain in the gable area.

Accordingly, phosphorus does not explain the facts related in the evidence.

(b) *The Magic Lantern Theory*

A person may have concealed himself and his apparatus somewhere near the church and projected the images on the wall. For some time after the apparition this seems to have been the possibility most talked of and the one most carefully and scientifically examined. No less an authority than Dr Lennon, Professor of Science at Maynooth College, travelled to Knock for the purpose of carrying out tests with the specially constructed camera. His visit shows that the magic lantern theory was being taken seriously, and that the possibility was being thoroughly investigated. Dr Lennon was by no means prejudiced in favour of the apparition. His opinion on this matter is based entirely on his expert knowledge and the investigation he had made.

The following are the considerations that are to decide the question:

(i)   Dr Lennon's opinion is as follows: 'That [this] means was used I think highly improbable; indeed I may say, morally speaking, impossible – keeping in mind some statements of the witnesses, the position of the building, the part illuminated and the facility of detection by even the most ignorant.'

(ii) MacPhilpin writes: 'The nearest point at which a performer could stand is thirty yards from the gable, and no lens and no electric light known to scientists at the present day can cast fully defined likenesses the size of a man on four hundred square feet of space for some hours in the light of day, and the darkness of night, and that with pencil rays of light invisible from artificial sources of illumination.'[9]

(iii) Had the figures been cast by a projector the witnesses who were standing in front of the gable would have cast shadows on the wall, and the figures which were only about eighteen inches above the ground would have been eclipsed. There is no mention of shadows or blacking-out of the figures in the evidence of any of the witnesses. The figures were visible all the time the witnesses were present.

(iv) It was raining heavily all during the apparition. Even in modern times it would be difficult, if not impossible, to project clearly defined pictures in the open air through heavy rain.

(v)   A beam of light from a projector would cause the rain to sparkle and appear more visible at night than in the day time. Rain is clearly visible in the lights of a motor car. One of the

wonders of the apparition was that no rain was seen to fall
where the light was.

(vi) It was still daylight when the figures were first seen and they
then appeared as statues standing by the wall. No projector
could produce images in the day time that would appear as
statues to observers who were viewing from an angle and three
hundred yards distant.

(vii) Mrs O'Connell described the tests carried out by the priests
with the magic lantern. The apparition was altogether
different from the pictures produced by the lantern. 'They
wanted to make out,' she said, 'that the pictures were like the
ones we saw, but they were no more like them and no one
could make them like the apparitions.'[10]

The apparition, therefore, as described by the witnesses,
could not have been produced by magic lantern. The question
of magic lanterns will be discussed further in Chapter 10,
'Other "Apparitions"'.

III. Imagination

Two kinds of imagination disorder can cause people to think they
see what in reality they do not see:

(a) Illusion

(b) Hallucination

(a) *Illusion*[11]

An illusion is the mistaking of a real object for something other
than what it is. The real object is deformed or transformed in the
mind of the seer by a false association of images. Thus if a person
says he saw the hands of a statue move, or the eyes of a painting
turn from side to side, there is a possibility that the person is
suffering from an illusion. In the Knock apparition the witnesses
were not mistaking ordinary statues for a supernatural
manifestation, because there were no statues there. They did
think at first that what they saw was an array of ordinary statues,
but when one of them tried to kiss the feet of one of the figures

she found nothing. As well as having her own word for this we have the testimony of several others of the witnesses who corroborated that she tried to put her hands around the figure. Mary Beirne declared she heard the woman say, 'Níl tada annseo'. We can take it, then, that there were no statues or similar objects there to lead to a false interpretation.

The possibility of deception due to alcoholic drink could come under the classification either of illusion or hallucination. For the sake of convenience we may discuss it here. It was known that Mary McLoughlin, the priest's housekeeper, had on occasion taken alcoholic drink, and it was said that sometimes she took too much. This got much publicity in the years following the apparition, and many critics concluded that the whole apparition could be explained in that way; namely, that Mary McLoughlin was under the influence of drink on that night, that she imagined she saw something, and that she induced others to see what she saw.

What are the facts?

(i) Several witnesses saw the apparition independently of Mary McLoughlin. Margaret Beirne saw the light over the gable early in the evening. Patrick Walsh saw the light after darkness had fallen. Mary Beirne testified in her 1879 deposition, and confirmed in 1936, that she had heard nothing of the apparition from Mary McLoughlin until she saw it herself. Mary McLoughlin, therefore, had said nothing about the apparition she had seen until several others had seen it themselves.

(ii) On the night of the apparition Mary McLoughlin was not under the influence of drink. Mrs O'Connell was asked about this by the 1936 Commission. She replied: 'She was as good a housekeeper as ever a priest had, but she had a little fault.' The doctor had allowed her some drink and 'she got into the habit for a short time of taking more than enough. But that evening she had no more sign of drink than I have now.'

The alcoholic theory, therefore, is contrary to the evidence and cannot be admitted as an explanation.

(b) *Hallucination*

Hallucination differs from illusion in many ways. Hallucination is an organic or functional disorder of the brain by which, without any external cause, a mental state is excited and internal images are formed in such a way as to have the appearance of real objects. Psychologists distinguish between 'true' and 'pseudo' hallucinations. The true or sensorial hallucinations 'create an appearance of objective reality' and are 'vivid, animated, exact, stable, spontaneous and incoercible'.[12] The pseudo hallucinations create images, but in such a way that the subject can recognise that his experience is hallucinatory, because it is 'lacking in that character of exteriority which [is] inherent in sensorial hallucinations'.

It will not always be easy to distinguish between a hallucination and a vision. The problem is particularly difficult when there is question of the experience of a single person. Hallucination and a vision differ objectively in that the former does not arise from any external object, whereas the latter is caused in some special way by God. But on purely psychological grounds it is said that it is usually difficult, and sometimes almost impossible, to distinguish one from the other. Theological and other extrinsic considerations will have to be invoked. Although this particularly difficult problem has confronted investigators in the case of other extraordinary happenings, the problem as it presents itself in the case of Knock is simpler and less difficult. For here we are concerned not with the experience of a single person but with the experience of several people.

If there is hallucination, therefore, it will be mass hallucination, and mass hallucination raises fewer and less difficult problems than does the hallucination of a single person. Second, assuming that the occurrence at Knock was preternatural, it would appear that it was an apparition rather than a vision. In a vision, although God plays a special part in the production of the concept or image, there is no external correlate present to the beholder. In an apparition, on the other hand, there is an external correlate for whose presence God is in some special way responsible. The senses of the beholders of an apparition are acting normally. At Knock several people saw the same thing. All who came to the scene saw what was to be seen immediately on their arrival. The evidence leads one to believe that there must have been something external to see. If there was nothing external, then, assuming still that the experience was preternatural, the only alternative is that God acted on each person separately; there would have been a multiplication, apparently without need, of cases of direct divine intervention, and this would be contrary to the economy of divine action. In the present context, therefore, the case resolves itself into making a decision as to whether the occurrence at Knock was mass hallucination or an apparition. If it was not mass hallucination, it must have been an apparition, as all other possibilities have now been eliminated.

Investigations have shown that in some cases where a crowd of people has come under a collective hallucination there has been a wide divergency in the images seen by the several individuals, but it is also established that in some cases of extraordinary happenings experienced by a crowd of people there has been substantial uniformity in the individual accounts, and yet in those cases the supernatural could not be admitted as an explanation. Psychologists do not profess to be able to explain all the natural forces that may lie hidden in the human mind. It is admitted, at any rate, that certain happenings which in former centuries might be regarded as miraculous are now being taken as possibly natural. That is not to say, however, that we can never know whether any particular phenomenon is supernatural or merely natural.

There are certain criteria which, when applied, can give certainty, or probability, in varying degrees according to the nature of the evidence available. In the present inquiry it is proposed to apply tests – physiological, intellectual and moral – for the purpose of deciding whether mass hallucination may be admitted as an explanation of the happenings at Knock.

(1) Physiological Test
(i) Hallucinations in general may be caused by disease of the brain or nervous system. They may also be caused by intense expectation or desire in people of a certain temperament. A frequent characteristic of mass hallucination is that the imaginations of the several individuals are stimulated beforehand by common emotions, and the 'imaginations are successively awakened by a kind of mutual provocation of those who saw first'.[13] Are any of these characteristics present in the story of the Knock apparition?

The witnesses of the Knock apparition were ordinary, hard-working country people. They were of sound mind and normal behaviour. Their mode of living and open-air life kept them close to reality. There is no trace of disease of the brain or nervous system in any of them. One of them was said to be 'a little bit odd', but that was of no great consequence and, in any case, several had seen the apparition before he saw it.

What of the expectancy and desire? Were they under the influence of some great excitement? It will be remembered that more than a year before the apparition the church had been wrecked and the statues in the church broken. New statues were broken in transit. Finally, two statues were got from Lourdes, one of which was that of Our Lady of Lourdes. Dr Lennon comments that 'the subject of apparitions, like those at Lourdes, had evidently been much talked about in the neighbourhood', and that the breakage of the statues on the way to Knock must have attracted much attention and deep regret.

Was the Knock apparition due to any previous talk about Lourdes or to feelings of emotion arising from the incident of the statues? In reply to this it is to be observed that, whenever preoccupation with the thought of an apparition excites a person to the point of suffering hallucination and 'seeing' another apparition, the effect produced is no more than a poor or clumsy imitation of the original. The Knock apparition is not an imitation of Lourdes or of any other known apparition. Second, let us consider the facts of the happening at Knock: Margaret Beirne had locked the church and saw an unusual light over the church, but it never entered her head to investigate. Mary McLoughlin saw figures and thought they were new statues. Mary Beirne saw the figures and at first thought they were statues. Mrs Hugh Flatley on seeing the figures thought they were statues. Patrick Walsh, from half a mile away, saw a great light over the church, and thought some people had made a fire near the church. All these were independent witnesses; none of them was influenced by anybody else in noticing what was to be seen. There had been no excitement that day; the rain made the surroundings singularly uninspiring. There was no excitement at the time of perception; there was no common emotion, expectancy or desire of the supernatural. The witnesses' behaviour was normal; their interests were ordinary and commonplace. Each of those who first saw the figures, on adverting to something unusual, automatically supplied in his or her own mind a natural explanation. The incidence of the breaking of the statues, far from leading them to think of a supernatural vision, caused them to think that what they saw was natural, until they were convinced they were not looking at statues. Some of the witnesses watched the apparition for over an hour. They went away for a short time, and returned full of desire and expectancy to see the apparition again. But on their return there was nothing to be seen. Expectancy and desire were unable to reproduce what they had witnessed.

It matters little, therefore, whether the people of the locality had sometime beforehand discussed apparitions or not, or whether they had been grieved at the loss of the broken statues; the evidence shows that on the evening of the apparition they were not thinking of apparitions or the supernatural. The idea of an apparition was forced on them by what they saw.

It is true that on the very day on which the apparition was seen at Knock, 21 August 1879, an impressive ceremony had taken place at La Salette, in which the statue of Our Lady was solemnly crowned by the Papal Legate, the Cardinal Archbishop of Paris, before a vast assembly of bishops, priests and lay people. Nobody in Ireland at that time seems to have adverted to the coincidence. It was not mentioned by Dr Lennon, nor was it mentioned by any of the critics of the time. We can take it, therefore, that the ceremony had not been published in Ireland, and that it could not have been known to the people of Knock.

It cannot, then, be said that the apparition at Knock was due to diseased mind or expectancy or desire or common emotion.

Coming to the question of mutual suggestion or provocation we find that the first four witnesses who saw the figures at the church gable, and Patrick Walsh who saw the light from a distance, all saw what was to be seen independently of one another. None of these five, at least, was influenced by any of the others in seeing what was to be seen. Of particular significance is the fact that Patrick Walsh was about half a mile away. There could not be any possibility of his being included by those present at the church. The amount of his evidence recorded by the commission is small, but there is reliable oral testimony that, when he returned to his home from the land on that night, he declared to the members of his family that there was a great fire burning in the church yard, and he expressed surprise that anybody should light a big fire so near the church. What he saw was different from what the people at the gable saw. Yet, what he saw fully fits in with what the others described.

(ii) Substantial divergencies in the several accounts of witnesses would indicate hallucination. There are divergencies in the testimonies of the Knock witnesses but not of a substantial nature. The witnesses are in agreement in regard to the substance of the apparition and nearly all the details. Such minor divergencies as occur strengthen rather than weaken the evidence, as they are an indication that each witness is anxious to tell his or her story as they saw it. Differences of this kind are to be expected. Several people who witness the same football game will have some divergency in describing what they saw.

(iii) If the sense of vision can be checked by some other sense, especially that of touch, we have a circumstance strongly favouring the reality of the apparition. Many of the witnesses stated that, though it was raining heavily at the time, no rain fell where the figures were. Mrs Trench felt the ground carefully with her hands and it was perfectly dry. There is no reason to doubt the truth of the evidence of the witnesses who testify on this particular point.

(iv) A feature frequently found in mass hallucination is that some of the crowd do not see anything. Others do not see anything at first, but do so later. At Knock all the witnesses saw what was to be seen. They saw it immediately on coming to the gable. They were no longer able to see it when they departed. Their visual experience had the characteristics of vision of objective reality.

It emerges from these considerations that certain characteristics commonly associated with hallucinations are absent from the happenings at Knock, while other characteristics, which one would expect in a real apparition, are present. The seeing of the light from a distance, and the feeling of the dry ground, as added considerations, leave the possibility of mass hallucination as inadmissible.

(2) Intellectual Test

Intellectual signs of hallucination are features that are extravagant, ridiculous or entirely lacking in inventiveness. If an apparition does not show any of these features, if it is regular, reasonable and harmonious in design, and if it expresses a lofty ideal, there is good ground for considering that it is not hallucination. The imagination can reproduce past experience; in reproducing it can combine elements experienced at different times, but it cannot create. If the apparition expresses an ideal which surpasses the knowledge of the seer in his or her normal state, and if it displays a knowledge of which the seer could not have been in possession by reason of his own ability and education, we have then proof not only that the apparition is not hallucination, but that it cannot be explained by natural causes, that it must be preternatural.

Let us examine the Knock apparition in the light of these principles. First, one can say that it contains nothing that is extravagant or ridiculous. Second, an examination shows that the arrangement of the several elements is regular, reasonable and harmonious. For example, the figure of Our Lady is on a higher level than that of the other two. The altar, lamb and cross are in the centre of the gable and on a higher level than the three figures. It may be said that the individual elements of the apparition are conventional. The figures were sufficiently conventional to enable the witnesses to recognise them. They all recognised the central figure as that of Our Lady, yet it cannot be said that the appearance of Our Lady was exactly like what the witnesses would have already seen in statues of Our Lady. The statues of Our Lady commonly seen in Irish churches were the image of the Madonna and Divine Infant, the Lourdes statue and the statue of Our Lady of the Miraculous Medal. In the apparition the crown on Our Lady's head, the upturned eyes and the position of her hands were features that would have been unfamiliar. It is said that the representation of Our Lady in the Knock apparition was very similar to a painting of her found in the Roman catacombs. It can hardly be said that such a painting would be known at Knock. The figure of St Joseph was easily recognised too, but his special pose was something original. Only one witness expressed opinion on the identity of the third figure, because of a statue she had seen in Lecanvey church. The statue in Lecanvey represented St John the Evangelist as holding a book in his left hand and having his right hand raised. There was no mitre on the statue in Lecanvey. There was a mitre on the figure in the apparition, 'not a high mitre but a short set kind of one'. John Curry describes it in 1937 as 'a little round hat'.

The lamb was a frequent symbol in Christian art. In the Old Testament the sacrifice of the Paschal Lamb pre-figured the Sacrifice of Our Lord Jesus Christ on the Cross. When Our Lord was on earth St John the Baptist pointed him out to his disciples saying, 'Behold the Lamb of God, behold Him who taketh away the sins of the world'. In the Mass we pray saying, 'Lamb of God who taketh away the sins of the world have mercy on us'. St John the Evangelist had a vision of heaven which he describes in the Apocalypse:

'And I saw in the right hand of him that sat on the throne, a book written within and without.

'And I saw: and beheld in the midst of the throne and of the four living creatures, and in the midst of the ancients, a Lamb standing as it were slain, having seven horns and seven eyes: which are the seven spirits of God, sent forth into all the earth.

'And I beheld, and I heard the voice of many angels round about the throne, and the living creatures, and the ancients; and the number of them was thousands of thousands.

'Saying with a loud voice: The lamb that was slain is worthy to receive power, and divinity, and wisdom, and strength, and honour, and glory, and benediction.' (Apoc V, vv. 1, 6, 11, 12)

In the Christian art which flourished in the early centuries after the conversion of Constantine the symbols of the cross and the lamb were used to denote the Holy Victim of Calvary. In a sixth century mosaic of the Vatican Basilica a lamb is represented as standing on a throne at the foot of a cross studded with gems. From the side of the lamb blood flowed into a chalice, from which it again flowed in five streams, representing the five wounds of Christ. There is preserved at Ghent a famous fifteenth century painting by the Van Eyck brothers representing the adoration of the Lamb as described in the Apocalypse. The Lamb, throne and cross differ in some aspects from the representation at Knock. In the apparition the lamb is not looking towards the people; he is facing towards the figures, while there is a wealth of other details surrounding the central theme of the painting which is entirely absent in the scene at Knock.

The combination of lamb, throne and cross would have been familiar to students of Christian art. The witnesses at Knock may, or may not, have seen reproductions of one of the early masterpieces. Even if they did, the representation in the apparition is not an exact reproduction of the works mentioned. Each of the constituent elements of the apparition, then, is conventional to an extent, but the combination, as far as we know, is original. The individual elements are conventional in some aspects, but they also display features that were new and unfamiliar. These original features are not wanting in inventiveness, but are such as to bring a unity of design and harmonious arrangement to the whole tableau.

Does the apparition express an ideal? No words were spoken but an examination of the tableau reveals a definite symbolism. The figure of Our Lady was the one which most attracted the witnesses. Her hands are in the position in which a priest holds his hands when celebrating Mass. Her eyes are raised to heaven. She is, therefore, in a position of prayer, intercession, mediation. Her crown symbolises her Queenship, and presupposes her Assumption into Heaven. St Joseph was on Our Lady's right. In 1870 Pope Pius IX had declared St Joseph Patron of the Universal Church. In the apparition he is in the attitude of one paying honour to Our Lady, but his joined hands also symbolise prayer and petition. In heaven his prayer is for the Universal Church. On Our Lady's left is a figure of St John. He is wearing a mitre; he has a book in his left hand; his right hand is raised; he is in the attitude of one preaching. Mitre, book and preaching symbolise the teaching of the Church. By his right hand this figure is drawing attention to Our Lady, and by being partly faced the other way he is also drawing attention to the altar, lamb and cross. The lamb and cross are a recognised symbol of the Victim of Sacrifice. The third figure, therefore, is drawing attention to the mediation of Christ. An inference seems possible and reasonable. Our Lady intercedes for the Universal Church. She is Queen of Heaven and Mediatrix of all graces. Her mediation, however, is efficacious only through the merits of Christ's mediation on Calvary which is made present again in the Mass.

To sum up the character of the apparition, we can say there is in it nothing that is ridiculous or extravagant; it is regular, reasonable and harmonious in design. It expresses an idea. The idea presupposes an understanding of scripture and theology and sacred art beyond the knowledge and capability of simple, uneducated people such as the witnesses. Not only would it be impossible for such an apparition to be the result of hallucinations, but due regard being taken of all the circumstances and the condition of the witnesses, it is reasonable to conclude that the designing of the tableau of the apparition cannot be explained by natural causes: only a cause higher than natural can supply a satisfactory explanation of the facts.[14]

In regard to the timing of the apparition it may be relevant to mention that the year 1879 marked the Silver Jubilee of the Definition of the Dogma of the Immaculate Conception. August 21 was the eve of the Octave of the Assumption, and on the very day of the apparition, 21 August 1879, a statue of Our Lady was solemnly crowned by a Papal Legate at La Salette. If we take these circumstances into consideration, the apparition at Knock combines many of Our Lady's prerogatives: her Immaculate Conception, her Assumption, her Queenship and her Universal Mediation.

There are some circumstances which might be considered adverse intellectual signs:

• No words were spoken; no verbal message was delivered.

Two objections arise under this head:

(a) In other apparitions Our Lady declared who she was. Since no words were spoken at Knock, how could any of the figures be identified?

It will be conceded that God is not limited in the means he may adopt for revealing the identity of heavenly visitors. The resemblance of figures to the conventional notions of heavenly beings seems an adequate means for revealing identity. The central figure of the Knock apparition was so like the conventional notion of Our Lady that none of the witnesses had any hesitation in saying it was she. The same is true of the figure on Our Lady's right. All took him to be St Joseph. 'Anyone could know St Joseph,' said Mrs O'Connell. Difficulty arises in regard to the third figure. St John the Evangelist was not a common subject in ecclesiastical art. Few people would have any definite notions as to what he looked like. Of the fifteen witnesses, there was only one who remembered seeing a statue of St John. She had seen it in Lecanvey church. The statue in Lecanvey had a book in the left hand and the fingers of the right hand were raised. It was this 'coincidence of figure and post' that made Mary Beirne surmise that the third figure was that of St John. The surmise seems reasonable, and the resemblance between the statue and the figure could be accepted as intended by God for revealing the identity of the third figure.

The mitre does not afford much help for identification. Actually none of the Apostles would have ever worn a mitre. However, if St John or any other Apostle were to appear on earth, there is no intrinsic difficulty in believing he could appear wearing a mitre. He would thus be conforming to the present-day notion of the liturgical head-dress of a bishop. But the mitre in the Knock apparition can convey no more significance than that the figure was that of a bishop; it does not afford evidence that the figure was that of St John. If we are to seek confirmation of the view that the figure was St John, we may find it in the argument for appropriateness. The altar, lamb and cross have a decided resemblance to the vision of heaven described by St John in his Apocalypse. If St John were to appear on earth in order to convey a message on the Redemption, by means of a symbol, it would be fitting for him to use the symbol which had already become associated with his name. Second, St Joseph and St John were, next to Our Lord, the two most closely associated with Our Lady in her mission as Mother of the Redeemer and the Second Eve. Of all the saints she might have chosen to accompany her to deliver a message on Redemption, the two that would seem most likely for selection would be St Joseph and St John. Because St John stood by the Cross on Calvary he was associated in a special way with Our Lady in her mediation.

The circumstantial evidence supporting the view that St John was the third figure is, therefore, considerable, and as there is little or no evidence to lead one to surmise that the figure was that of any other saint, we may reasonably conclude that the third figure was St John the Evangelist.

(b) No verbal message was delivered.

Various methods of communication have been used in revelations[15] (i) intellectual locutions: the pure expression of an intellectual idea without the aid of any word or image; (ii) imaginative locutions: composed of words not heard by the ear but received directly by the imaginative sense; (iii) auricular locutions: heard by the ear as in natural speech; (iv) messages delivered by writing. The first two methods have been experienced by people far advanced in the mystical state. Instances of the third and fourth methods are to be found in the Bible. None of these methods was used at Knock.

Is it possible for a message to be delivered in any other way? What of a message by symbols? It is reasonable to draw conclusions from symbols that in the mind of people of a certain place or time have a definite connotation. The silent figures of the Christmas crib have for centuries embodied a sublime message for people of all ages and nations. The early Christians used symbols to express truths of the Christian Faith. Our Lord himself taught much of his doctrine in parables. The parables were stories about ordinary happenings, yet they held a deeper message which people were expected to interpret by their reasoning powers. Delivering a message by symbols, therefore, is an accepted and reasonable method for communicating information.

If we are to seek a reason why the message was not delivered in one of the other ways, an answer may be found first in the fact that the witnesses at Knock had no mystical experience during the apparition, and so the first two methods were excluded. Second, a message given by either of the last two methods would have to be given in two languages, in both Irish and English, if it were to be intelligible to all the witnesses.

To suggest that Our Lady might have used the gift of tongues as the Apostles did on Pentecost would have necessitated an additional miracle, and miracles are not multiplied needlessly. It would also render the witnesses more exposed to the criticism of sceptics who would see in the one message heard by different people in different tongues a strong reason for suggesting hallucination. Finally, it can be asked would a verbal message or an inscription have been more effective than the symbolism of the Knock tableau? It is doubtful. The symbolism of Knock, as interpreted, is rich in meaning, and its full explanation would fill many pages. It can be argued that the silent pose of the figures is as eloquent as a message in words.

- It seems strange that the witnesses did not acquaint the parish priest of the apparition.

The evidence given is that his housekeeper, Mary McLoughlin, left the scene of the apparition to tell him. In her 1932 statement Mary Beirne says the following: 'Mary McLoughlin, housekeeper to Archdeacon Cavanagh, went to the parochial house to acquaint the parish priest of the occurrence. He, however, did not visit the scene, believing, as he told his housekeeper, that it was a reflection from a stained-glass window erected some time before.' MacPhilpin quotes the Archdeacon on this as follows: 'Inferring that the vision had disappeared, and omitting to question my housekeeper on that point, I did not go up, and I have regretted ever since that I omitted to do so.'[16]

Nobody else went to inform the parish priest. All the others would have been aware that the housekeeper had gone in to the parochial house. If he did not want to come out they would consider that was his business, and it was not likely that any of them would take it upon themselves to tell the parish priest his business. Besides, all the witnesses lived in the immediate vicinity of the church, and they did not summon anybody from the direction in which the priest's house was situated.

In other apparitions Our Lady manifested herself only to one or a few favoured persons. Even though others were present at the scene, they were not enabled to see Our Lady. At Knock, all who came to the church gable saw the apparition. It is possible that Our Lady could have wished a certain number and no more to see the apparition. If she did not wish the priest or others to see the apparition, the most reasonable way of not allowing them to do so was to ensure that they did not come to the church gable. Had the Archdeacon seen the apparition, it is likely that some critics would use that fact as an argument against its authenticity. Later, as we shall see, when Archdeacon Cavanagh was enthusiastically promoting the cause of the shrine, many people charged him with credulity, and pointed to this as an unfavourable circumstance. The fact that the priest did not see the apparition cannot be considered an argument either in favour of, or against, authenticity.

• The witnesses departed from the scene while the apparition was still visible. It seems strange that people who believed they were looking at heavenly visitors should go away while the visitors were still there.

From the evidence it is clear all did not go away for the same reason, or at the same time. Mary McLoughlin went away to inform the priest. Others were standing there for over an hour and were drenched with rain. John Curry stated before the New York tribunal: 'The reason we left was it was teeming, pouring rain and we were all wet.'[17] John Curry was in the company of Dominick Beirne (senior), Patrick Hill and John Durkan. There is no reason to be scandalised at their departure in the circumstances. Though they were full of amazement and wonder at what they saw, they were not in ecstasy, and they were not insensible to prolonged discomfort. People who go to adore the Blessed Sacrament exposed on the altar do not feel they are showing any irreverence if they depart after an hour's adoration. Mary Beirne was in the last group to leave. They were summoned away by a sudden alarm. Of this Mrs O'Connell says: 'I think they all went away when I went away. They went to where there was an old woman dying whom they thought was dead, but she wasn't dead. Her daughter was down and said she was dead, but it was only a faint. She died next day.' The details of this story were well known in the Knock locality. Mrs Campbell is the old woman mentioned here. She it was who made an attempt to leave her sick bed and see the apparition. Her daughter, Judith Campbell, was one of those at the church gable, and she on her return, finding her mother unconscious at the door, thought she was dead. When she called the others they ran to her assistance. They were away about ten or fifteen minutes. When they returned, the apparition was no longer to be seen.

When all things are considered, the behaviour of the people cannot be considered unreasonable. In fact they seem to have acted in due accordance with Christian Charity. Our Lord has said: 'As long as you did it to one of these my least brethren you did it to Me.' (Mt XXV, 40) Had the people ignored the appeal of Judith Campbell, it could be said that they were subordinating the law of Charity to their own selfish satisfaction, and far from being an argument in favour of the divine origin of the apparition, such behaviour, instead, would be a strong argument against it. As things happened, the witnesses showed true Christian instinct.

(3) Moral Test

The third kind of test is that based on moral signs. The intellectual tests show whether an apparition is from a source outside this world – whether it is preternatural. The moral tests decide whether the source be good or bad, divine or diabolical. It is recognised that the devil can at times perform wonders, and for a time deceive people. The signs belonging to the moral order are drawn from three principal sources: the person of the witness, the mode of the apparition and the effects which it produces.

(i) *The person of the witness*

Of this Fr Poulain writes: 'Experience seems to prove that God has at times manifested Himself to simple souls of quite ordinary virtue, in order to found a pilgrimage or to suggest some useful undertaking.'[18] 'History proves that visions or exterior locutions have often been received, transiently, at any rate, by persons who were still in the way of ordinary prayer,' and he adds, 'The apparition to the children at La Salette would seem to be a case of this kind.'[19]

It does not seem possible to doubt that the witnesses of Knock fulfil this condition. They could be taken as displaying a cross section of Irish life. Some were very devout; some were constant in ordinary piety, and some few, perhaps, had their ups and downs. The witnesses of La Salette also were said to have had moments of inconstancy. Mrs O'Connell, who was the most important witness, lived to be eighty-six years old, and she was always exemplary through her long life. Sr Mary Francis Cusack had this to say of Dominick Beirne (senior): 'He was considered by his neighbours as rather a hard-headed character, and by no means likely to be carried away by a vision. Some time later in the evening when the apparition had passed away, he lifted his hat reverently and said: "Well, I never knew how good I was till now." One cannot but smile at the simplicity of the remark, but there lay underneath a deep reverence.'[20]

The reputation of the witnesses in general was that they were good-living Catholic people.

(ii) *The mode of the apparition*

An apparition of divine origin is recognised by its dignity, goodness, holiness. From the analysis already made in another context it is evident that the Knock apparition possesses these qualities. Sometimes the devil apes God and disguises himself as a holy being, but God will not allow him to make a perfect reproduction. There will always be some ugly feature to betray the wicked mind. There is nothing in the Knock apparition that could be considered as indicating that the devil had any hand in it.

(iii) *The effects of the apparition*

The most notable effect was the growth of pilgrimages to the shrine. These started immediately after the apparition, and have continued up to the present time. Everybody agrees that pilgrims coming to Knock displayed, and continue to display, extraordinary piety and devotion. Nobody denies that these pilgrimages have fostered devotion to Our Lady in a remarkable way. The effects are so praiseworthy that it does not seem possible that they could have come from the devil. They can be attributed only to a holy source.

The moral tests, therefore, based on the character of the witnesses, the mode of the apparition and the effects show that the apparition could not have been from the devil.

The application of the three tests – physiological, intellectual and moral – show that hallucinations do not explain the apparition, and that a supernatural cause is the only reasonable one.

Finally there is a test of special significance – that of miracles.[21] A miracle offers proof of the divine origin of an apparition in the following cases: (i) when the apparition itself is accompanied by phenomena which are miraculous; (ii) when the apparition states that a certain miracle to be performed is a sign of its origin; (iii) when no explicit statement is made, but when circumstances show that a miracle is to be accepted as a sign of divine origin.

A miracle is an effect perceptible to one or other of the senses, produced outside the course of nature and explicable only as an act of God. To prove that a miracle actually took place there must be a witness or witnesses who recognised the event, and there must be proof that the effect was due to a supernatural cause. The qualities required of a witness are that he be able to recognise the event, that he have the use of his senses and that he give sufficient attention to what is happening. In regard to proving the supernatural cause there are cases where it can immediately be declared with certainty that the effect transcends the powers of nature, e.g., raising a dead person to life, or the suspension of the law of gravity. There are also cases where it is difficult to know with certainty whether the effect is beyond the power of nature or not. Cures from certain kinds of ailments would come within this category. To know where nature ends and where the supernatural begins in these cures requires expert knowledge.

Before the Church recognise a bodily cure as miraculous, certain conditions must be fulfilled. The certificates of medical experts are required to show that a disease really existed, that the cure took place, that the cure could not be explained by any natural cause.

Were there any miracles at Knock? With regard to the apparition itself several of the witnesses stated that, though it was raining heavily during the apparition, no rain fell where the figures were. This could not be due to the shelter of the gable wall, as the wind was coming from the south. The witnesses were in a position to recognise the facts, to know where rain fell and where it did not. No expert knowledge was required for that. A beam of light makes rain sparkle at night time and more obvious than in the day. Had rain been falling in the area of light where the figures were, the witnesses could not have missed seeing it. They noticed rain did not fall here, and they were surprised. The visual experience was confirmed by Mrs Trench: 'I felt the ground carefully with my hands and it was perfectly dry.' The preventing of the falling of rain in that area seems to be a suspension of the law of gravity, and does not admit of a natural explanation. A miracle accompanying the appearance of an apparition would prove the divine origin of the apparition itself.

What of other miracles? The apparition did not declare that any miracle would be performed, but are there any miracles which, from the circumstances of their performance, could be regarded as a sign of divine authentication?

Many extraordinary cures have been reported at Knock

from the year of the apparition down to the present time. Archdeacon Cavanagh kept a diary of cures in which over three hundred cases were recorded. In modern times a long list was prepared by Liam Ua Cadhain and published in his book, *Knock Shrine.* In the year immediately following the apparition many crutches and surgical appliances were left at Knock by invalids as evidence of cures. The use of cement from the apparition gable was said to have miraculous power, and many cures were claimed to have been wrought by its application.

What are we to think of all these reported cures? It must be noted at first that the records mentioned here are not official. Second, it is obvious at first glance that many of the cures in Archdeacon Cavanagh's diary could readily be explained by natural causes alone. If each of the crutches and surgical appliances left at Knock church represented a miraculous cure, the number of miracles would have been very great, but evidence given before the 1936 Commission makes it fairly certain that many of the crutches and appliances were left there by invalids who hoped to be cured on arriving home.

Notwithstanding all these cases, where a miracle was obviously excluded, it cannot be denied that there are very many cures listed which on their face value seem to be very extraordinary, if not miraculous. The trustworthiness of the people claiming the cures, the good faith and extreme care of the compilers render them all the more credible.

The great difficulty that has beset investigation of cures at Knock is the want of medical certificates. In the last century few Irish people who claimed cures at Knock had such certificates. Some were unwilling to have themselves examined by a doctor after a cure, as they felt a medical examination would be tantamount to doubting the reality of their cure, and might cause a recurrence of the disease. A commission was set up in 1882 by Archbishop McEvilly to examine cases of cures. No report, not even in copy, of this commission is extant. We do not know what cures they investigated or how many. Archdeacon Fallon, who succeeded Archdeacon Cavanagh as parish priest of Knock, stated before the 1936 Commission that he had seen the report years before, and that the substance of it was that the commission could not declare that any of the cures examined by them was effected by supernatural agency. As we do not know what cases they examined, and as we have no records of their investigations, the commission of 1882 affords no grounds on which to form a conclusion one way or the other.

The 1936 Commission examined witnesses for eight reported cures. It also took statements from Dr George Maguire, Secretary of the Medical Bureau founded in 1935 by the guild of SS Luke, Cosmas and Damian. Dr Maguire stated that up to that time (September 1937), in a period of more than two years, the Bureau had examined nineteen cases. Three cases did not easily admit of a natural explanation. One was sufficiently contrary to ordinary clinical experience to make the case a very remarkable one. No statement was made by either the Bureau or the commission on any cases investigated.

This concludes the inquiry. Let us now sum up the findings. All possible natural explanations were discussed: deliberate falsehood on the part of the witnesses; deception by means of phosphorescent paint or magic lantern; illusion; hallucination. It was found that none of these cases gave a satisfactory explanation of the apparition.

The passing of the years since 1879 has afforded circumstances which have reinforced the evidence. In all those years nothing has been discovered to discredit the story of the witnesses. The devotion of the people of Knock has continued without interruption from the beginning. That it survived the unhappy events of the eighties is remarkable; that it endured for many decades without any sign of official favour and in face of clerical indifference and opposition is more remarkable still. Since 1929 the devotion has grown to proportions greater than ever before. There have been no abuses in the history of the devotion; on the contrary, the piety of the pilgrims and the worthiness of the devotion have never been questioned. It is agreed that the Knock Shrine devotion fosters and promotes devotion to Our Lady. These circumstances in the history of Knock Shrine provide additional evidence in favour of the divine origin of the apparition.

Positive Signs

The Church Commission of 1879 reported that 'the testimony of all, taken as a whole, is trustworthy and satisfactory'. There is no doubt about the truthfulness of the witnesses.

In the eyes of the witnesses the apparition was beautiful, holy and from heaven.

The design of the apparition presupposes an understanding of scripture and theology beyond the knowledge of the witnesses. The depth of the scriptural meaning of the apparition together with the other positive signs shows that divine origin is the only satisfactory explanation of the apparition.

This conclusion is confirmed by other considerations: the images were standing about eighteen inches above the ground where there was long grass; the standing images did not cause the grass to bend; this shows that the images were not statues. Another important sign was that, although it was raining heavily at the time, no rain fell on the images. This was a miraculous suspension of the law of gravity.

Finally, the wonderful spiritual benefits bestowed by God on the ever increasing numbers of pilgrims taking part in the devotions at Knock Shrine is a continuing sign of the divine origin of the apparition.

9.

After the Apparition

The inquiry has brought us to events that occurred many years after the apparition. Let us return to 1879. The news of the wonderful happening spread quickly, and pilgrims were coming in greater crowds every day to throng Knock church and its surroundings. Invalids too were brought there, and many miraculous cures were being claimed. As it was said that the cement from the apparition gable had wonderful powers, and as many cures were claimed through its use, the cement itself was eagerly sought by all pilgrims. Soon the gable wall was so stripped that it was in danger of collapsing, and the parish priest was obliged to put a protective covering of boards on the whole lower portion of the gable to prevent further damage to the building.

Because of the desire of the clergy that no widespread publicity be given to the reports of the apparition, the newspapers made no mention of the story for several months after the apparition was seen. The first report to appear in a newspaper was given in the *Tuam News* of 9 January 1880. Shortly afterwards the Dublin *Weekly News* began a series of detailed articles on Knock. The London *Daily Telegraph* sent a special representative to write the story, and several other papers also carried long accounts of the apparition and the crowds and the extraordinary cures.

John MacPhilpin of the *Tuam News* visited Knock in person. Among other things, he has this to say: 'The West of Ireland at the present moment presents an extraordinary attraction of a higher kind to not only natives in Ireland, but to all Catholics in these kingdoms, as well as to their brethren on the continents of Europe and America. A second Lourdes has arisen at Knock, a small village surrounded by little hills. The multitudes who flock to the chapel, or Catholic church at Knock, from the surrounding districts are quite as numerous as those that formed the monster meetings, which, for the past nine months, have been held in the counties Mayo, Galway and Sligo.'

The *Daily Telegraph* writes: 'Mondays and Thursdays are the times when Knock is overwhelmed with pilgrims, many thousands being frequently present at once; but on no day of the week is the place deserted … It is needless to say that the [gable] wall itself, boarded though it be, excites the utmost reverence. I saw a score of people kneeling before it repeating prayers, some of them knowing the spot on which they believe the Virgin appeared; while others had brought sick children, upon whom they lavished attention in the intervals of devotion. Others again wandered round and round the chapel, telling their beads as they went – an act of Faith, so I am assured, altogether self-imposed. Yet others, mostly afflicted with diseases, stood about in the road, or enclosure, waiting, like some at the Pool at Bethsaida long ago, "for the moving of the waters". Night and day they wait, filling the chapel during the dark hours, and praying there so as that the sound of their voices can be heard far down the road.'[1]

The *Weekly News* gives long and detailed reports. Here is one: 'Arriving at the cross-road of Knock, we found it no easy matter to make our way to the chapel, past the post office at the corner and the half-dozen straggling cottages that constitute the village. A line of vehicles was drawn up at either side of the road, and the space between was filled up by people on foot, continually moving to and fro. Although Mass had long been over, the church was crowded still to the very doors. It was difficult to get in, and all but impossible to get out. Before the statue of the Blessed Virgin, to the left of the altar, a number of candles were lighting, and here the deep hum of fervent prayer subdued all other sounds. So absorbed was I in observing the tokens and signs of spiritual fervour that it was only when I stumbled into a hole in the clay floor of the humble church that I noticed that there were several of these shallow excavations. Little by little they had been made by the people, who took away small quantities of the earth. Going round to the southern gable, I found that since last week, it had been sheathed with planking to a height of about eight feet from the ground. This was necessary in order to save the wall, for the people first of all had stripped away the cement; then they had picked out the mortar from the spaces between the stones; and at last the stones themselves had been taken out of the wall, and two large holes were left through one of which a man could almost enter. The parish priest had to resort to the expedient of plank-sheathing in order to save the wall from going, stone by stone. When I came in sight of the gable, there were several men and boys, propped up on the shoulders of the crowd, detaching with knives and crook-handled sticks small particles of the cement above the sheathing, while hats were held out below to receive the tiniest fragment that might fall. Around the gable, and all the way down to the girls' school at the southern end of the enclosure, the space that had been five months ago – at the time of the first apparition – occupied by a waving meadow, and that up to a few days since had been dry and smooth and grassy, was now covered with a paste of mud to the depth of two or three inches. Thousands of feet had come there laden with the mud of the reeking highway, and multitudes had come and gone upon the surface of the enclosure, till every blade of grass disappeared, and in place of a dry and smooth expanse there was left a place torn up as if a pitched battle had been fought upon the scene. At every step the foot sunk ankle-deep. Yet all who approached the gable knelt, and many prostrated themselves in audible or silent prayer. No ordinary consideration was allowed to check the fervour of the pilgrims. And not alone in the church and the enclosure surrounding it were the people absorbed in prayer, but away in the field beyond the schoolhouse wall, and in that separated from the road by the church enclosure; away beyond the line of booths, and standing or kneeling by hedgerows at a distance, were to be noted numerous groups and many solitary figures engaged in telling beads or reading prayer books. The spirit of devotion was intense and all-pervading. I never, in all my life, beheld a spectacle so thrilling, by reason of the intensity of its religious fervour and the majesty of its spiritual exaltation. I do not anticipate that I ever shall see the like of it again.'[2]

As the years passed, feastdays of Our Lady became days of special devotion at Knock, and May, August and September were the busiest months. The Feast of the Assumption was the biggest pilgrimage day of the year. The first organised pilgrimage consisting of fifty members of the Confraternity of the Holy Family came from Limerick in March 1880. In June (Feast of the Most Pure Heart of Mary) a pilgrimage organised by the Dominican Fathers came from Cork. A second pilgrimage of 500 members of the Limerick Confraternity came in August 1880, and a second one from Cork about the same time. In 1882 a pilgrimage of 900 members came from Manchester.

The devotions that became popular were the Rosary and the Stations of the Cross. The Rosary was recited aloud by groups 'doing the rounds' of the church outside. The practice of 'doing the rounds' at shrines in Ireland dates from the time of St Patrick. It is interesting to note how it was automatically adopted by the pilgrims at Knock. All-night vigils were kept on the eves of important Feasts of Our Lady – the all-night vigil on the eve of the Assumption being the one that attracted a particularly large gathering. On the occasion of these all-night vigils especially, pilgrims were anxious to go to Confession and receive Holy Communion. It can be said in general that the devotions practised at Knock were spontaneously adopted by the pilgrims. The candlelight procession held on the anniversary of the apparition was, however, introduced by Archdeacon Cavanagh. Records show that all visitors to Knock, whether they were sceptics or believers, were deeply impressed by the extraordinary piety and devotion of the pilgrims.

Knock was honoured by the visits of some distinguished

pilgrims. In 1892 Archbishop Lynch of Toronto made a pilgrimage to Knock in thanksgiving for a favour received. He presented a banner to Knock church with the inscription, 'Toronto is grateful'. After his visit to Knock he wrote to a bishop in Canada a letter which is of interest, and of which the following copy is taken from Sr Mary Francis Cusack's *Three Visits to Knock*.[3]

'My dear Lord – On Friday morning, the 9 inst., I left Dublin for Claremorris. I was met at the station and most hospitably entertained by the Very Rev. Canon Bourke, parish priest of that place. As I was somewhat discouraged to go to Knock by some people who never saw the place, I determined to interrogate sharply the good Canon before I would proceed further on my journey, or, rather, pilgrimage. The Very Rev. Canon was Secretary to the Ecclesiastical Commission of Investigation appointed by the late illustrious Archbishop of Tuam to inquire into the reported apparitions and miracles of Knock. The present Archbishop, Most Rev. Dr McEvilly, the worthy successor of the late Archbishop McHale, assured me lately at Maynooth College that Canon Bourke was a gentleman of very great ability, piety, prudence and learning, so I was prepared to abide a good deal by the information which I should receive from him. He assured me that fifteen witnesses of different ages and sexes and quite worthy of belief were interrogated apart from one another, all giving the same testimony as to the apparitions, none in any essential particular differing from the rest, so that as far as human testimony could go it was conclusive. On earth we need not expect any other than human testimony, as the angelic is seldom vouchsafed. It cannot be supposed that all these persons either combined together to invent a falsehood and stick to it, or that all were under the same hallucination, and conceived that they saw at different times what did not exist.

'Then, as regards the miracles, many were fully proved. I did not care to interrogate about the miracles, as we had many of them in Toronto ourselves. After dinner we took a carriage with the Very Rev. Canon, and two lay gentlemen, friends of mine, and drove to Knock, about six miles and a half distant. Alas! on the road I was saddened to death at seeing a number of cabins deserted, with the doors roughly walled-up with cobble stones. The land around appeared to be of the worst kind, and was left untilled. Eighteen poor families were recently evicted from these miserable cabins and bad land. The scene of desolation was most oppressing, and the more so when we considered the sufferings of the poor former inhabitants of these cabins. I visited a neat wooden cottage such as you would see in America built on a safe piece of ground for a poor evicted family, by the charity of the people through the Ladies' Land League, without whose help thousands would have perished of cold and starvation. The children were some of the most graceful and beautiful I ever saw. They were evicted from the place of their birth and childish happiness. I thought that it was a most merciful condescension on the part of Our Immaculate Mother to appear in the neighbourhood of such a place, and to give the patience and courage of saints and martyrs to these poor people who had to bear a cross – one of the heaviest that could be imposed on a father, mother and children – to be driven from their homes by no fault of theirs, but because in the mysterious ways of Providence, three bad harvests had deprived them of the means of paying their rents. I have been told by their parish priest that these poor people left their homes as quietly as Saints, resigned to the will of God, but praying to the Holy Mother for patience and another home.

'With a heart depressed by the thought of human depravity, and consoled in turns by the thought of human virtue, and praying that these poor people might be comforted by the Almighty God in their affliction, we approached the church of Knock. We came first in sight of the gable upon which the apparitions appeared. A vast number of crutches and sticks lined the walls, and another lot stood in a sort of a pen in the chapel yard. We felt greatly moved at that venerable place. There is a marble statue of the Blessed Virgin in the attitude and in the place where she was seen by the crowd of people, old and young, on 21 August 1879. This statue was presented by a pious lady in Dublin, and statues of St Joseph and St John are expected to be presented by some devout clients. There is a very fine iron railing around the ends of the church to prevent the pilgrims from again removing the plaster from the gable; the old plaster was taken down and preserved, and also given to pilgrims from all parts of the world, and like the water of Lourdes, performs wonderful cures, according to the faith and fervour of the people who use it. The things that are not, God makes use of to confound the wise of this world. The surroundings of the church have been so often described that I need not say anything about them. We entered a venerable church, which is large and imposing with a magnificent marble altar, the gift of another servant of God.

'After adoring the Most Blessed Sacrament, and invoking the intercession of the Holy Mother of God, St Joseph and St John, we took another view of the church. The venerable Archdeacon Cavanagh, who had been hearing Confessions, came to salute us. He is a quiet, unassuming priest of middle age, tall and thin, and ascetic looking, and well calculated to make a favourable impression on all who approach him. This is another stroke of the holy Providence of God to have such a priest in so celebrated a place that the pilgrims may carry away besides other gifts a great reverence for the priesthood of Ireland.

'We returned to Claremorris the same evening, calling at the Presentation Covent,[4] near Claremorris, to see the good nuns of the Presentation Order and Sr Mary Francis Cusack, formerly the "Nun of Kenmare", who resides with the nuns till she can build a convent of her Order at Knock. A convent there is much needed for the reception and instruction of other female pilgrims, and I hope there will be also a monastery with a hospice or lodging-house for the men, for in the neighbourhood there are but few hotels, and the crowds of pilgrims betimes is very great. There are such establishments at Lourdes, at Lough Derg, and other places of pilgrimage. The Convent of the Presentation is situated delightfully in the midst of an ancient forest, with a wide road leading to it through over-topping trees. The house appears about 200 years old, large, and commodious. I had the curiosity to inquire who built it or lived in it. One of the last occupants was called the priest-killer, from the number of priests that he hunted down or killed in the old penal times. Time has its revenges, and the Holy Sacrifice of the Mass is now offered up where a priest would be killed by English law for doing so, and especially if the former owner of that house caught him. Sr Mary Francis Cusack is collecting funds for her future convent, and awaiting the orders of her ecclesiastical superiors to commence the work. We have sent our little contributions towards the good work to the Archbishop of Tuam that we may have a share in the graces that Our Good God and Our Blessed Mother are giving to the holy place of Knock. Next morning at half-past six o'clock we again left Claremorris for Knock, and at eight o'clock we commenced Mass, offering the Holy Sacrifice for ourselves, clergy, religious and people committed to our care, for we seldom offer the Holy Sacrifice for ourselves alone. There were a few hundred people at Mass, the pilgrims as well as the people from the neighbourhood. I gave the Communion to about thirty. The fervour which appeared on the countenance of the people and their attention at prayer were very edifying. I said a few words to them exhorting those who lived in the neighbourhood to honesty, sobriety and holiness, so as to leave no bad impression on the pious pilgrims who came to visit the holy shrine which is in the midst of them. I spoke to only one witness of the apparition. The young man made a good impression on me. I did not come to investigate, but to pray. I was satisfied with the account of the investigation already made, which is published in a small volume, and sold at Gill & Sons, Sackville Street, Dublin. About the same number of cures and improvements are recorded here as at Lourdes, about 10 per cent, but it is to be hoped that all go away to bear the Cross which Our Lord refuses to take from them. A few imaginary cures have been related, and some relapses also, and on that account the real cures are denied by the incredulous. All this, of course, is not surprising, nor should we be surprised if some of the nine lepers who were restored to their health by Our Lord got again a touch of the leprosy for their ingratitude. St Peter, also, began to sink in the waves for either too much or too little confidence. The followers of Thomas, before he was truly converted by the descent of the Holy Ghost, are, of course, to be met with everywhere. They are now our would-be scientists, who explain away every miracle – that Lazarus was only in a trance, that the cure of those that were thrown into the probatic pond was effected by the sudden dash into cold water, etc. Our Lord said: "Though you do not believe Me believe My works," so I would say that the works performed at Knock speak enough for those who are prone to believe. The most extraordinary objection was, I presume, said in a joke, that Archdeacon Cavanagh's piety and fervour in the cause rather hinder than hasten the recognition of the wonders of Knock. Yet the testimony and fervour and enthusiasm of one little girl at Lourdes, in France, did not hinder the recognition of the apparition of the Blessed Virgin. The testimony of a crowd of witnesses, and the piety and enthusiasms of the Archdeacon of Knock supported by many well-authenticated miracles, should be at least on an equal footing with those of Lourdes.

'The ecclesiastical authorities will, of course, imitate Rome in its slowness in giving its solemn decision on the wonders of Knock, but that slowness is not intended to disprove the apparition or to operate against the devotion of the people or the power of the Blessed Virgin. We recollect how much discussion and divergence of opinion there were about the apparition of La Salette and of Lourdes, but time cured all these, and will, I hope, act in the same manner with respect to Knock.

I am &c., &c.,
† John Joseph Lynch
Archbishop of Toronto'

Another distinguished visitor was Archbishop Murphy of Hobart, Tasmania.

'On Wednesday evening, the Most Rev. Dr Murphy, Bishop of Hobart Town, Tasmania, Australia, with his Vicar-General, the Most Rev. Dean Beechinor, arrived at Knock and stayed at Churchfield Hotel. Dr Murphy said the eight o'clock Mass next morning, and Mass being over addressed the assembled worshippers. He spoke of his having come 16,000 or 17,000 miles to return at Knock his thanks to the Mother of God for the exceeding favour done to him by the restoration of his sight through the agency of the cement from the church of Knock. So impaired was his sense of vision that he had to cease his recitation of the Divine Office. A Sister of Charity in Hobart Town who had received from Archdeacon Cavanagh some of the precious cement gave some to His Lordship with the above happy result. Dr Murphy further informed his auditory that the cures wrought by the Knock cement in Australia were more than numerous. In the afternoon of the same day Dr Murphy and Dean Beechinor left for Tuam.'[5]

Of Archbishop Murphy's visit Mrs O'Connell said: 'I also remember well Archbishop Murphy who came on a visit of thanksgiving. One day at the gable wall he addressed those of us gathered there and told us to pray with great confidence that it was not the "statue" but Our Lady herself that had come there and that he himself was cured through her intercession.'[6]

Archbishop Murphy presented an oil painting of the apparition to Knock church.

Archbishop Clune of Perth stated he had obtained a cure through the intercession of Our Lady of Knock and presented an oil painting to the church in thanksgiving.

10.

Other 'Apparitions'

The apparition which we have been discussing took place on 21 August 1879. Official cognisance was taken of it by the Archbishop of Tuam, and it was investigated by an ecclesiastical commission. Several other apparitions were reported as having taken place at Knock in the first three months of 1880. No official notice was taken of these by the Archbishop, there was no official investigation, and the information we have on them is derived mostly from press reports of the time. It is recognised that after an apparition one must be prepared for what is called 'spiritual mimicry'. Not only is it possible that the devil may try to act as 'the ape of God', but human beings also, whether through malice or unconsciously through involuntary deception, may try to reproduce the original apparition. Such mimicry does not affect the reality of the original. 'Imitations being a counterfeit of the true, far from destroying or rendering doubtful the idea of a true, it presupposes and confirms it, as a copy requires an original. ... The first vision, or series of visions, alone has the right to escape suspicion of mimicry.'[1] The mimicry usually manifests itself in a clumsy imitation of the original, and can easily be unmasked through the application of the recognised tests.

Several unusual occurrences at the south gable of Knock church were reported during the months of January and February 1880. The *Weekly News*[2] interviewed a Miss Anderson, one of the witnesses of the appearance on the night of 5–6 January. Her story was that she and a Miss Kennedy saw a strange appearance on the gable of the church on the night of 5 January. They came to the church at about eleven o'clock on that night, 'because', as she said, 'it was the eve of the festival, the eve of the Epiphany, and we were in the hope of seeing something'. They saw nothing at first, but she continues: 'We came to the gable of the school and we knelt outside it and said the Rosary. Mrs Killeen, a woman of the village, called our attention to the gable of the church. Then I saw, on the side of the gable towards the road, a row of lights along the wall, from the edge of it to the direction of the window … scattered up and down the gable in several directions there were numerous other lights the same as those in the row … there were frequent changes. The lights used to fade slowly, until they got very dim, and then they used to brighten out again, but they never got very bright … after a time I saw other lights like stars; they appeared as if coming out at different parts of the wall … after seeing the light and stars, I saw, lower down near the ground, a small figure, about a foot and a half in height. From the appearance of the head and shoulders I took it to be a figure of the Blessed Virgin.'

Two policemen were also interviewed.[3] Sub-Constable Fraher gave information as follows: 'Sub-Constable Collins and I were out together on duty. It was just about twelve o'clock when we reached the chapel. As we passed it by on the road we heard the voices of people praying aloud, not in the chapel, but outside it, near the gable. We went in to find the cause of the people being there. At first we saw nothing particular. After five or ten minutes I observed a row of lights extending across the wall of the gable … I saw other and brighter lights appear suddenly on different parts of the wall. One of them would shine out, dash along the wall, and disappear. Then after two or three minutes, another would come in a different part of the wall, and it would disappear in like manner.' He saw no stars and nothing like a statue or human figure. Sub-Constable Bernard Collins gave similar evidence. He, however, stated he saw one star. 'It remained some time, and then it vanished suddenly. It was small and very brilliant – dazzling.' He was asked if the appearances could have been produced with some instrument by a person hidden somewhere about the place and he replied: 'The light was not like any light produced by such a means. Besides I searched behind the schoolhouse wall, and behind the other walls and through the fields about. I searched the whole place as closely as if I was looking for a thief, and there was no one to be found.'

Another appearance was seen on 10 February. John McCloskey of Claremorris was witness. His evidence is given by MacPhilpin:[4]

'I, John P. McCloskey, a native of Claremorris, remember the night of 9 February, and the morning of 10 February. Simon Conway, MacGeoghegan and I left Claremorris at ten o'clock p.m. We arrived at Knock sometime after midnight; our desire was to behold the apparition. After we had arrived, we continued to pray for some time. At about three and a half o'clock on the morning of 10 February, while I was praying before the gable of the Knock chapel, I saw a light, like a white silvery cloud, move in a slanting direction over from where the cross stands, on the apex, and overspread the gable. In this white cloud I saw distinctly the figure and form of the Blessed Virgin Mary, so clearly and fully that I perceived the fleshy colour of the feet. Her dress resembled that made of white satin, and it contained numerous folds. The light had hardly settled on the gable when it began to grow less bright, and to seem to fade or darken in colour, leaving a wreath of its own brightness still around the head of the Blessed Virgin, while the rest of the gable became the colour of white paper stained with pencil strokes. Every now and then a red tongue of flame used to shoot down from the heavens and cross the gable. During the momentary brightness resulting from these flashes, the figure of the Blessed Virgin was each time fully seen. In the absence of such flashes she was seen too, but not so distinctly, only in subdued tones of colour.

'What attracted my attention to the gable at first was small stars of an emerald clear greenish colour, that appeared to go in and out through the gable, and at different parts of it. A star continued at intervals to twinkle right over the region of the Blessed Virgin's heart, and a little group of four or five stars were seen on the left side of the head. At no time did I see the countenance of Our Blessed Lady so clearly and distinctly as to be able to describe accurately the feature or the expression of the face. It was usually shrouded in light, and only at certain moments did I get a glimpse of full features.'

The *Daily Telegraph*, February 1880, reports Archdeacon Cavanagh as saying: 'I shall ever feel sorry that a sight of the apparition has been denied me … Though I have not witnessed the divine manifestation, I have seen the light, and once when standing at some distance from the church, in company with others, a most brilliant star flashed along the gable leaving a train of radiance.'[5]

An Examination of the Reports

Many people believed these appearances to be supernatural and a confirmation of the original apparition of 21 August 1879. In the absence of any diocesan intervention it may be useful to examine in some detail the statements of the witnesses quoted in press reports of the time. It is to be noted that the subject of the 1879 apparition was in the minds of the people of Knock and of the pilgrims coming there. Witnesses of the 1880 appearances stated they came to the church in the hope of seeing something or of seeing an apparition. The times of the appearances are also significant. On the night of 5–6 January lights were seen around midnight; on 10 February about 3.30 a.m.; and on 12 February about 8.15 p.m. All these appearances were seen during the hours of darkness.

The Lights

The witnesses place special emphasis on the lights. On the night of 5–6 January lights were seen moving upwards and downwards and from left to right. Lights appeared suddenly on the gable wall and then disappeared. Lights failed until they got dim and then brightened out again.

Of special significance is the evidence given by the two policemen who were out together on duty and arrived at the church just about midnight. It would seem that their only interest was in doing their duty as policemen. There is no mention by them of any desire on their part to see an apparition. Yet they did say that they saw the lights. This may be taken as reliable evidence that the lights were real. A suggestion was put to one of the policemen that the lights could have been produced with an instrument by a person hidden somewhere. He replied that the lights were not like any lights produced by such a means. Besides, he said, he searched behind the walls near the church and through the fields about, and the whole place very closely and there was no one to be found. It may be accepted that the policeman made the search in the manner described. However, the lights may have come from a distance beyond the limits of the search. The ground in that area slopes gradually from the gable wall of the church down to a hollow, and rises from the south side of the hollow to a level higher than the ground level of the church. More than one policeman would have been required to search thoroughly all that area on a dark night in January. Moreover, a hidden operator would have chosen a position that would be as secure as possible from detection. The most secure position would have been on the high ground south of the church. The darkness of the night would be helpful for the testing of lights. It would also be useful for avoiding detection.

The lights themselves have no discernible meaning. The fact that they were focused on the gable wall of the church would indicate an attempt to reproduce the apparition of 21 August 1879. The mechanical and fitful movements of the lights suggest that they were being produced by a person hidden somewhere with an instrument such as the so-called magic lantern. The dimming and fading and disappearing of the lights would suggest a defective instrument or an inexperienced operator. Or perhaps a skilled operator was designedly using an instrument in such a manner as to confuse or bewilder the spectators. The appearing and disappearing of the lights and the other strange movements of different kinds of lights would keep the spectators in a high state of expectation of seeing something wonderful. They would not look behind to see where the lights were coming from. They would keep their eyes fixed on the church gable wall.

The witness who saw the lights at 3.30 a.m. on the morning of 10 February describes some new features. He says he saw a light move in a slanting direction from the apex of the gable. The slanting direction suggests a beam of light coming at an angle from a position not in a direct line from the church. Every now and then, he says, he saw a red tongue of flame that used to shoot down from the heavens and cross the gable. This in turn caused repeated flashes of momentary brightness. The whole scene could have had the effect of a small fireworks display and would have caused great excitement in the witness. In themselves the lights were without meaning.

The brilliant star seen at about 8.15 p.m. on 12 February and 'leaving a train of radiance' would have been just another special effect from a hidden source.

To sum up – the lights as seen on dates in January and February 1880 and as described by the witnesses bear little or no resemblance to the light seen at the church gable on 21 August 1879. This was a light illuminating the gable wall and all the figures, and remaining constant for a period of about two hours which included some daylight time and some night time. The repeated attempts in January and February 1880 to reproduce this light can reasonably be described as a failure.

The Figures

The witness who saw the lights at about midnight on 5–6 January also saw low down near the ground a small figure about a foot and a half in height which she took to be a figure of the Blessed Virgin. The two policemen who were on duty that night saw the lights but nothing like a statue or human figure. Their evidence can be accepted as reliable. In any case the vision of a figure a foot and a half in height would be ridiculous.

The appearance on the morning of 10 February requires careful examination. A witness and two friends left Claremorris at 10 p.m.

on 9 February and arrived at Knock after midnight. Their desire was 'to behold the apparition'. The use of the definite article could have referred only to the apparition of 21 August 1879. They prayed and waited at the church gable until 3.30 a.m. Then one of the witnesses describes what happened. The greater part of his statement is taken up with a description of the spectacular performance of the lights. He describes only one figure. His description of that figure is brief. For this, the reader is referred back to p. 112.

Comments

The light 'like a white silvery cloud' resembles a description given by Judith Campbell, a witness who gave testimony before the Diocesan Commission after the apparition of 21 August. In this testimony she states: 'All the figures were in white, or in a robe of silver-like whiteness.' With regard to the figure, the 1880 witness says: 'I perceived the fleshy colour of the feet. Her dress resembled that made of white satin, and it contained numerous folds.' At no time did he get an accurate view of her face. The details he gives of the figure are insufficient to enable one to say whose figure it is. With the meagre description he gives, the figure is unidentifiable. Furthermore, the details he does give bear a decided resemblance to some of the evidence given by some of the witnesses of the apparition of 21 August before the Diocesan Commission. It is sufficient to give an extract from just one of those witnesses. Patrick Hill, of Claremorris, states in part: 'I distinctly beheld the Blessed Virgin Mary, life size ... clothed in white robes ... The robes came only as far as the ankles; I saw the feet and the ankles; one foot, the right, was slightly in advance of the other.' The resemblance between these two statements of the 1880 witness and the testimonies of Judith Campbell and Patrick Hill on the 1879 apparition is of such closeness as to lead one to believe that the 1880 witness had read the testimonies of the witnesses of the 1879 apparition published in the *Tuam News* in January 1880. A further comment about these details would be that they are of lesser significance in comparison with the other and more significant details given of the figure seen and described by the witnesses of the 1879 apparition – the prayerful position of the hands, the eyes turned towards heaven, the brilliant crown on the head, and over the forehead a beautiful rose. These were the details which enabled the witnesses of the 1879 apparition to identify the figure they saw as that of the Blessed Virgin Mary. There is no mention of these details in the figure seen on 10 February 1880. Neither is there any mention of the other two figures, nor of the lamb, altar and cross.

Other relevant observations must be considered also. The witness tells of the circumstances preceding the happenings at Knock – his leaving Claremorris at 10 p.m. on 8 February, his arriving at Knock church after midnight, his desire to behold the apparition, the long hours of praying, waiting and hoping until 3.30 a.m., the sudden appearance of the spectacular light which he believed to be miraculous – all these circumstances were such as to cause a pious pilgrim to be filled with emotional and elated excitement which could cause his imagination to slide out of control and to believe he was seeing what he desired to see. This is the process that is called spiritual mimicry. In this case there was a combination of the active and passive elements of deception; a person or persons hidden somewhere performed the active part with an instrument such as the magic lantern, and a witness experienced the passive part in being deceived by the lights and his own imagination into believing he was seeing a real apparition. Examples of this phenomenon have taken place after apparitions on the continent of Europe. It should be no surprise that spiritual mimicry happened at Knock after the apparition of 21 August 1879.

Finally, 'the red tongue of flame and the flashes of brightness' described by the 1880 witness were somewhat theatrical, undignified and unbecoming of the apparition of the Blessed Virgin Mary.

The figures as described by the witnesses in the press reports of the January–February 1880 occurrences at Knock church display no more than failed attempts to reproduce the apparition of 21

August 1879. The results can fairly be described as a travesty. No blame can be attached to the witnesses. They were deceived by a person or persons unknown. 'Imitation being a counterfeit of the true, far from destroying or rendering doubtful the idea of a true, it presupposes and confirms it as a copy requires an original ... The first vision, or series of visions, alone has the right to escape suspicion of mimicry.'[6]

All those so-called apparitions of 1880 got wide publicity, and were offered to the public in unofficial publications as being worthy of credence. Some writers seemed to put the 1880 occurrences on an equal footing with the apparition of 1879, and make no distinction between them. It is not to be wondered at, if the public mind was confused on the story of Knock because of the uncritical reporting of happenings, and the mixing of the genuine with the counterfeit.[7]

The Letters from Belfast – Tuam Diocesan Archive

A letter was received by Archbishop Thomas Gilmartin of Tuam from Fr James P. Clenaghan, St Malachy's church, Belfast. It was dated Corpus Christi, 1936. In the letter Fr Clenaghan writes that on the preceding day a parishioner, Mr Michael McConnell, called with him to make a statement. In the statement the parishioner relates that many years beforehand an old Catholic policeman had told him that he had joined the force in the 1870s and that his first appointment was in Knock. Mr McConnell quotes the policeman as saying:

'In the barrack where I was, there was a Protestant policeman who was experimenting with lime-light which was just then being developed. He succeeded in throwing lime-light figures from the barrack window to the wall of the church. Some people saw the figures and thought them miraculous. Some short time after, he repeated the experiment – with the result that there were crowds and more talk and discussion. Then he became alarmed lest he might be found out. He applied for a change and asked the other men in the barrack not to give away the story on him.'

Several objections could be raised against the story. The evidence it contains is hearsay; it dealt with events that took place fifty-six years earlier. It was never investigated by a Church Commission or by any known Police Enquiry. The Protestant policeman was not named. The story contained nothing more than unsubstantiated allegations. However, for the sake of argument, the story may be examined at face value. It must be stated that the story cannot be accepted as referring to the apparition of 21 August 1879, for the reasons given in Chapter 8 in the section under the heading 'The Magic Lantern Theory'. The part of the story that deals with experimenting with lime-light could refer to the lights that witnesses claimed to have seen on the church gable during January and February 1880. The claim made in the letter that the policeman succeeded in throwing lime-light figures from the barrack window to the wall of the church cannot be accepted. The barrack was 400 yards from the church. It would have been impossible even with the best technology available at that time to project figures on to a surface 400 yards away.

Archbishop Gilmartin did not publish the letter. He would have several reasons for not doing do. He would have seen the flaws of the story. The publication of unsubstantiated allegations could, at that time, have caused offence to certain sections of the community. It was obvious that the story could not have referred to the apparition of 1879.

A second letter from Fr Clenaghan, dated 16 June 1936, addressed to Fr Fergus, Archbishop's Secretary, acknowledged receipt of Fr Fergus's letter dated 13 June 1936. In this letter Fr Clenaghan states that the incident related in his first letter was told to him by Michael McConnell. He said he met Michael McConnell on that day and told him 'to try to trace his informant – and whether he finds him or not, to write out his own account of the conversation'. He thanked the Archbishop for his prompt reply to his letter.[8]

Eleven years later Michael McConnell wrote a letter to Fr Clenaghan, dated 2 September 1947. A carbon copy of the letter is kept in Tuam Diocesan Archive. In this letter Mr McConnell names the 'old Catholic policeman' as Mr McDermott. We begin with the part of the letter that is relevant here. Mr McDermott is quoted as saying: 'there was an entertainment being got up in the parish and one of the items on the programme was lantern slides representing religious subjects. At that time there was a young man in the barrack who knew all about the working of a magic lantern, and although he was Protestant, it was arranged that he should take charge of the slides. When the lantern arrived, he decided to test it and see it was working properly, and one evening he trained it on the gable of the church and produced a good picture. It was this picture seen by the passers-by that gave rise to the report of the apparition. It was the whole talk of the place next day; the news spread near and far.'

The letter continues that 'the operator regarded this such a good joke that he repeated the picture on several occasions; then he became frightened when it dawned on him if it became known that he as a non-Catholic had been playing tricks things might become very unpleasant for him'.

The remainder of the letter states that the operator let the men in the barracks into the secret. He told them he would apply for a change and get away as quietly as possible. He asked them not to let him down. They assured him they would not let down a comrade. He got his transfer and slipped quietly away. The letter is signed by Michael McConnell.

Comments

The statement that 'an entertainment [was] being got up in the parish' raises immediate questions: who organised the entertainment? Where was it held? What was the nature of the entertainment apart from the lantern slides? What was the nature of the religious slides? Was the entertainment performed as planned? Did the policeman operator perform the role assigned to him? All these questions are unanswered.

If a public entertainment had been held in which lantern slides of religious subjects had been shown on a date before the apparition of 21 August 1879, it would have been publicly known in the area, and would certainly have been brought up by critics who did not believe in the apparition as an argument against the authenticity of the apparition. But no mention was recorded by any one about this alleged entertainment. No information is given as to whether the entertainment was performed as planned, or whether the policeman fulfilled the role assigned to him. The whole story of the entertainment lacks credibility.

The claim that the operator produced the apparition of 21 August 1879 when he was testing the lantern for the entertainment is preposterous. It contradicts the evidence given before the commission by the witnesses; it contradicts the judgement of the commission that the evidence was trustworthy and satisfactory; it contradicts the statement given by a Professor of Science that the apparition could not have been produced with a magic lantern.

Two weeks after the taking of evidence by the witnesses before the commission, that is, towards the end of October 1879, the Rev. Dr Lennon, professor of Science at the National Catholic Seminary in Maynooth, at the invitation of the commission, travelled to Knock for the purpose of carrying out tests with a specially constructed camera and slides to ascertain whether the apparition of 21 August could have been produced with these instruments. A large gathering of priests from outside Knock and some people from the Knock neighbourhood had gathered to witness the tests. In due course Dr Lennon sent his written opinion to the commission that producing the apparition with a magic lantern was 'morally speaking, impossible'. ('Morally speaking' means leaving no room for reasonable doubt.) Amongst those who saw the tests being carried out was Mrs Mary O'Connell, nee Beirne, who had seen the apparition on 21 August. With disdain she rejected the pictures produced by the lantern and slides as being anything like what she saw in the apparition: 'They wanted to make out,' she said, 'that the pictures were like the ones we saw, but they were no more like them, and no one could make them like the apparitions.'

Finally, the claim that the policeman operator could produce a 'good picture' from the barrack window on the gable wall of the church, some hundreds of yards away, and that this picture was the apparition of 21 August is ridiculous.

'The operator regarded this such a good joke that he repeated the picture on several occasions.' This statement reveals the time that the operator was 'playing tricks'. The apparition of 21 August was never repeated. The tests done by Dr Lennon were not a repeat. There was no report of any attempt to reproduce the apparition until January 1880. During dark nights of January–February 1880 there were several repeated attempts to reproduce the apparition of 21 August 1879. Many believed that the occurrences were genuine apparitions. They had been deceived by a person unknown. A letter from Belfast tells us that the person was an unnamed policeman stationed in Knock.

March 1880

Some appearances of a different nature were reported in March 1880. According to a newspaper report Knock church was packed for a vigil on a certain night in March 1880. A crowd of people 'with minds wrought to the highest pitch of religious excitement' had gathered in the church, 'the crowd being so great as to almost prevent movement of the arms'. Many men and women in the crowd claimed to have seen visions.

It is clear from the report that no priest was present on this occasion. Sometimes the church was left open during the night to give shelter to the people present. All the circumstances of the gathering and the excited atmosphere indicate there was nothing supernatural in the occurrences; rather would the indications be that here was an example of multiple delusions.[9]

'Pious Mimicry'

A description of other visions supposed to have been seen in Knock church on Good Friday 1880 is given in a letter sent to the *Weekly News* signed by 'Bridget Hough', and reprinted in G.P. Warren's book, *The Apparition of Our Blessed Lady of Knock*.[10] It can be accepted that Bridget Hough was a pious person meditating on the Passion and Death of Our Lord. But the meditations are such as could be found in a religious publication. The experiences that were personal to herself could not be accepted as apparitions. They would have spiritual value for the lady herself.

11.

Archdeacon Cavanagh

The parish priest of Knock was, in the minds of the people, closely associated with the apparition. The people of Knock considered that it was because of his sanctity that Knock was chosen for the favour of the heavenly manifestation. Bartholomew Cavanagh was ordained at Maynooth in 1846. His first appointment was to Westport where he distinguished himself by his piety, his great charity and his labours for the relief of the famine-stricken people. On being appointed parish priest of Knock and Aghamore in 1867 his piety and zeal found new scope. There was only one school in the parish when he arrived there. He established several others.

After the apparition of 1879 he attained a world wide fame and the people of his own parish had a greater reverence for him than ever. It became known after the apparition that he had completed one hundred Masses for the Holy Souls on the morning of the day of the apparition. Later in life, when he was ill, it was discovered that he had been wearing a hair shirt. His two great devotions were to Our Lady and to the Holy Souls. He died on the Feast of the Immaculate Conception, 1897.

The *Weekly News,* 1880, writes: 'The Archdeacon's residence stands about five minutes walk from the village and the church … No pastor in the land occupies a more modest dwelling. The low thatched roof, the rude white-washed walls, the few diminutive windows, all might lead the passer-by to look on it as the home of a small farmer, save for the low wall in front, the neat little gate, the narrow strip of grass separating the dwelling from the road. Here is the abode of a devoted ecclesiastic whose reputation for sanctity has spread far beyond the sphere of his ministrations.'

The *Daily Telegraph*, February 1880, reports him as saying: 'I shall ever feel sorry that a sight of the apparition has been denied me ... Though I have not witnessed the divine manifestation, I have seen the light, and once when standing at some distance from the church, in company with others, a most brilliant star flashed along the gable, leaving a train of radiance.'[1]

The Archdeacon showed great eagerness to gather all information concerning cures claimed at the Shrine. A notice was posted near the apparition gable which read: 'It is important that any miraculous cures wrought here would be made known to the parish priest.'[2] His diary of cures was entitled, 'An account of the miraculous cures wrought at the gable of the Chapel here, where the Blessed Virgin Mary, the Immaculate Mother, appeared on the night of 21 of August last'.[3]

His willingness to believe in visions and in miraculous cures caused adverse criticism. Archbishop Lynch gives a hint of this line of criticism in his letter where he says: 'The most extraordinary objection was, I presume, said in a joke, that Archdeacon Cavanagh's piety and fervour in the case rather hinder than hasten the recognition of the wonders of Knock.'

About the sanctity of Archdeacon Cavanagh there can be no doubt. We cannot be as certain about the reality of his visions. Several circumstances connected with his visions would argue for a natural explanation. He did not claim to have seen any vision before the apparition of August 1879. After that date everybody was talking of apparitions. Knock was the scene of continuous religious fervour, and Archdeacon Cavanagh himself was full of enthusiasm in favour of the apparition. He continued to fulfil his pastoral duties in his parish as devotedly as ever, and over and over this he was unsparing of himself in his ministrations to the continuous flow of pilgrims. It is possible that he suffered from strain due to overwork. From the accounts given it is obvious that he was of an unquestioning mind. The nature of his visions as described in the official accounts do not enable us to make a definite judgement on their origin. It seems a reasonable conclusion that it would be difficult to prove, from available evidence, that his visions were due to supernatural agency.

The reality or non-reality of Archdeacon Cavanagh's visions can in no way affect the reality of the 1879 apparition. Had he seen visions before that date, or had there been reports of visions seen by him, it could be argued that the people who saw the apparition were influenced by him. The reverse is the truth. When he was told of the apparition by his housekeeper, it made so little impression on him that he took no notice and did not believe. There is a story that during the 1880 apparitions a messenger was sent to him on a particular night to come out to see an appearance at the church, and that he replied he had no need to go out as he could see Our Lady in his own house. We cannot vouch for the story, but even if it were true, it has no bearing on the apparition of 1879. Neither can his willingness to accept stories of cures be advanced as an argument against what others had seen several months before. The fact that he listed cures that are obviously not miraculous does not preclude the possibility that some of the cures listed were in fact miraculous.

In fairness to Archdeacon Cavanagh it may be said that to a large extent it was people who were prejudiced against the apparition from the beginning, or who did not make a sufficient effort to investigate the facts, who devoted most attention to the uncritical faith of the Archdeacon.

12.

The Attitude of the Clergy

Some of the strongest opposition to Knock came from priests within the diocese and from others outside. It is estimated that at the time of the apparition, and for many years afterwards, the greater part of the priests of the diocese were sceptical and some were even openly hostile. The attitude of the successive parish priests of Knock was under special observation.

Archdeacon Cavanagh died in 1897 and was succeeded by Fr John Fallon, who showed no enthusiasm for the apparition nor hostility against it. According to his own evidence he did not question any of the witnesses. He was succeeded in 1909 by Fr John Corcoran. The people of the parish considered Fr Corcoran hostile. He had the crutches that were hanging on the inner walls of the church removed and burned. Fr Corcoran would have been aware that the greater number of those crutches had been placed there by people who had not been cured. Furthermore, the inside walls of the church could scarcely be considered an appropriate place for the display of the crutches. They gave the walls an unsightly appearance. Fr Corcoran was a man of taste who did much to improve the appearance of the church itself and its surroundings. The priests who knew Fr Corcoran would not consider him hostile to the apparition. One favourable sign was that he was always anxious to provide a large number of Confessors for the many pilgrims who came each year to Knock for the Feast of the Assumption. There is reliable evidence that before his death he professed his belief in the apparition.

It is not to be wondered at that priests should be the last to be convinced of the reality of an apparition. Their philosophical and theological training along with their studies in Church history makes them aware of the many possibilities there are of false visions and of the harm that such false visions can do to religion. In the interests of faith and morals they must be on their guard against deceit and imposture. Until such time as an authoritative decision has been made, the attitude of the clergy must be one of prudent caution. It is said that this attitude was accentuated amongst the Irish clergy by national temperament and more so by the conditions of the time. Through the persecution and for generations afterwards, the concern of the Irish clergy was to preserve intact the essentials of the Faith, and pre-occupation with this necessary duty gave them little time to devote to the 'extras'. The wide publicity given to unconvincing stories of apparitions said to have been seen at Knock in 1880 and afterwards was calculated to harden the clergy in their attitude of caution and criticism.

There is evidence that some of the criticism raised by members of the clergy against Knock was based on reasoning that was misinformed or not fully informed. Canon Grealy was asked by the 1936 Commission about objections he had heard from some priests, and in his reply he stated he did not consider them deserving of serious attention, and added: 'They were made chiefly by men who never investigated the case at all.' It can be admitted that many good and holy people, for aesthetic reasons, or because of temperament, are not attracted by popular devotions connected with private revelations, and feel unable to derive much spiritual benefit from them. Experience proves, however, that the messages contained in approved private revelations and the approved devotions connected with them are the means of immense spiritual good for the generality of the faithful. A divine manifestation is an effect of divine wisdom. Its effect is not to draw people away from real religion, but to draw attention in a very forceful way to some dogma of Faith, which is of special significance for a particular age.

In one sense an apparition can be regarded as a method of pastoral instruction. It gives a message that is to be accepted by the intellect, but it gives it in such a way as to stir the imagination and appeal to human sentiment. Many people, perhaps, may feel averse to the use of imagination or sentiment in instruction, and may prefer to depend on what may be called pure reason, but modern methods of pedagogy emphasise the usefulness of enlisting the aid of all the cognitive faculties for instruction; visual aids, coloured paintings and the story with a human appeal are all considered suitable methods for communicating ideas. For pastoral instruction it is recognised that the imagination and sentiment, when properly guided by reason, can be a powerful help towards moving the will to action. A real apparition can be used with remarkable effect for instruction and exhortation.

The opposition of the clergy, however explained, cannot in the circumstances be considered an argument against the apparition.

13.

The Archbishops and Knock

The ecclesiastical authority competent to make an official statement on the character of reported visions or apparitions is the bishop of the diocese. When an official inquiry has been conducted, the bishop may according to his prudent judgement follow one of three courses. He may give his approval to the apparition, stating that it is worthy of credence and that the faithful may prudently and with safety believe in it. A second course open after inquiry is what is called toleration, i.e., the bishop neither approves nor disapproves. The third course is condemnation; if the evidence shows that the apparition is certainly not supernatural, the faithful are forbidden to conduct pilgrimages to the place of the reported apparition or to practise devotions connected with it.

Dr McHale, Archbishop of Tuam, set up a commission in October 1879 to investigate the apparition reported on the preceding August. He died on 4 November 1881, at the age of ninety. When one considers the short time that elapsed before his death, and the condition of his health, one cannot reasonably expect that any definite pronouncement would have been made by him.

Dr McHale was succeeded by Dr McEvilly, who had been Coadjutor. His attitude to Knock was clearly stated in the letter addressed to the 'Nun of Kenmare' in which he gave his permission for a convent to be built at Knock. The following is the relevant extract: 'We would moreover, have it distinctly understood, that in thus acceding to your pious request, it is by no means to be inferred that we sanction or approve of the alleged apparitions or miracles said to have occurred at Knock. As at present disposed, we neither approve nor disapprove of such; we reserve our judgement until the time comes, if ever, for canonically and judicially investigating the whole matter. But at present we neither admit nor reject the alleged occurrences. So that we are in a position to approach the consideration of the subject with perfectly unbiased mind.'[1] The letter was dated 23 November 1881, and would have been written less than three weeks after the death of Dr McHale. Dr McEvilly did not set up any other commission to investigate the evidence for the apparition; it would seem he was accepting the report made by the commission in 1879, but in 1882 he set up a separate commission to investigate reported cures. The only information we have concerning the report of this commission is that it declared the commission could not pronounce in favour of supernatural agency for any of the cures examined.

Dr McEvilly ruled the diocese till his death in 1902, and made no pronouncement on Knock. The 1880 occurrences, the opposition of members of the clergy – these factors militated against a definite decision, and the Archbishop's attitude of neither approving nor disapproving seems to have been the most prudent one in the circumstances.

Dr Healy was appointed Archbishop in 1903. He ruled till 1918, and made no public pronouncement on Knock. But there is evidence as to what he thought of the apparition. To the 1936 Commission Canon Grealy stated: 'I heard Dr Healy speak about the matter and he said he saw no reason intrinsic or extrinsic why the apparition at Knock could not have been genuine.' Canon Grealy added that Dr Healy made this statement in answer to a person who was speaking in a disparaging way of Knock. Fr O'Connor who ministered at Knock from 1906 to 1920 declared before the 1936 Commission that Dr Healy used to like to see pilgrimages, and used to ask, 'Are they coming to Knock as numerous as ever?' Officially, however, Dr Healy maintained the policy of his predecessor – he neither approved nor disapproved.

14.

A New Era

For several years after 1879 pilgrims crowded Knock for a great part of the year. As the years passed, the number of pilgrims and the number of pilgrimage days were decreasing. By 1920 there was only one big pilgrimage day in the year and that was on the Feast of the Assumption. That day had always been since 1879 a day of great devotion at Knock. Many pilgrims anticipated the Feast by going to Knock on 14 August, and a goodly number kept all-night vigil at the church. The Feast of Our Lady's Nativity was also observed as a day of pilgrimage, but the numbers coming on that day were not as large as those coming on the Feast of the Assumption. Individual pilgrims and small groups could be seen on any day during the summer months. The causes for the decline in numbers of pilgrims may be found in the unfavourable happenings of the year following the apparition. What is most remarkable is that in spite of these unhappy incidents, and notwithstanding the hostility or indifference of the clergy, the pilgrimage tradition was preserved unbroken even in the most difficult years, and no year passed without its display of popular devotion.

What may be called the modern era of Knock began during the time when Fr John Tuffy was parish priest. Fr Tuffy, being a firm believer in the genuineness of the apparition, was anxious to make provision for pilgrims and to obtain official approval for the Shrine. When making some improvements in the church he issued an appeal in some of the newspapers for funds, and in a short time the amount needed was subscribed. In 1926 he petitioned the Archbishop of Tuam to approve a formula of devotions for pilgrimages.

In August 1929, on the Sunday within the Octave of the Assumption, Most Rev. Dr Gilmartin, Archbishop of Tuam, took part in pilgrimage devotions at Knock. The occasion was the first pilgrimage organised by St Michan's Conference of the St Vincent de Paul Society, Dublin. In an address the Archbishop referred to the commission of 1879 and explained that no authoritative decision had been made by the Church, and that a Catholic was entitled to follow his convictions in regard to the apparition. He made it clear that by his participation in the devotions on that day he was not thereby making any decision in regard to the apparition. Devotion to the Mother of God was independent of all shrines. He extended a hearty welcome to the pilgrims and praised their faith and piety. Even though the archbishop did not by his visit on that day give formal approval to the apparition itself, nevertheless, his participation in the devotions and his expression of welcome to the pilgrims implies a favourable attitude to the devotions connected with the Shrine, and presupposed that the evidence in favour of the apparition was good and worthy of consideration. It was an historic occasion, for it was the first time in which the Archbishop of the diocese took part in a pilgrimage to Knock, and the favour thus granted by him to the Shrine was received by the public with general satisfaction. From that day the number of pilgrimages to Knock was increasing each year.[1]

Fr Tuffy died in 1931 and was succeeded by Canon Grealy, who was equally enthusiastic for the cause of the Shrine. In 1932 the two witnesses of the apparition surviving in Ireland, Mrs Mary O'Connell and Patrick Beirne, were examined on the apparition by a board of priests. The evidence was sent to the diocesan archives in Tuam.

In 1935 a Medical Bureau was set up at Knock, with the approval of the Archbishop, by the Guild of SS Luke, Cosmas and Damian. The purpose of the Bureau was to offer expert assistance in the investigation of reported cures at Knock. The first President of the Bureau was Dr J. Stafford Johnson of Dublin, and its Honorary Secretary Dr George Maguire, Claremorris.

In August 1935 the Knock Shrine Society was established. The Society is composed of members of the laity. Its first president was William D. Coyne, District Justice. Its function was to help in promoting the cause of Knock Shrine. Two committees were formed, one of stewards and the other of handmaids. The stewards direct pilgrims in the formation of processions, arrange suitable order for outdoor public devotions, and attend to stretcher-case invalids. The handmaids attend to the needs of the sick pilgrims. Both stewards and handmaids give their services free, and they bear their own expenses for transport and meals.

In 1936 Most Rev. Dr Gilmartin set up the commission whose investigations continued for three years. In 1939 the report of the commission was sent to Rome by the Archbishop together with the request that a favour be granted to the Shrine by the Holy See.

While the commission was doing its work, improvements directed by Canon Grealy were being carried out in the church itself and its surroundings, and better facilities were provided for the benefit of pilgrims. As the numbers of pilgrims were increasing, and as the church building was inadequate to cater for the large congregations, provision was made for outdoor ceremonies. Outdoor Stations of the Cross were erected in the church grounds and blessed on 1 May 1938. In order to provide Mass and other ceremonies for the large crowds in the open air, an Oratory with sliding glazed doors in front was erected on the site of the apparition and dedicated to Our Lady of the Assumption on 5 May 1940.

Most Rev. Dr Gilmartin was succeeded as Archbishop of Tuam by Most Rev. Dr Walsh in 1940. From the beginning Dr Walsh actively participated each year in devotions and pilgrimages connected with the Shrine. On 9 May 1943, at Knock, he consecrated the Diocese of Tuam to the Immaculate Heart of Mary. It was the first diocese in Ireland so consecrated. In 1947 he authorised the Knock Rosary Crusade, the purpose of which is to encourage people to say the Rosary every day. He sponsored the cause of the Shrine and gave it his wholehearted support and approval. At his request the Holy See granted generous facilities for gaining Indulgences at the Shrine and gave permission to pilgrim priests to say a votive Mass of Our Lady at Knock on all except certain specified days. Furthermore, in answer to the Archbishop's petition, the Chapter and Canons of the Basilica of St Mary Major in Rome made the church at Knock an affiliated church of the Basilica of St Mary Major, with the effect that the church at Knock enjoys certain special facilities for Indulgences which are enjoyed by the Basilica of St Mary Major.

Bishops of other Irish dioceses too have come on pilgrimage to Knock. Several of the Irish diocesan pilgrimages are led by the bishop of the diocese. Cardinal D'Alton, Primate of All Ireland, visited the Shrine on 9 April 1953, and in an address said that Knock was the Shrine of the Blessed Virgin in Ireland. He hoped that devotion to the Mother of God would increase, and had no doubt that Our Lady's Shrine at Knock would do much to increase that devotion.[2]

Many bishops from other countries, especially America and Australia, have visited the Shrine in recent years. Several organised pilgrimages have come to Knock from America and some were led by a bishop. Cardinal Griffin, Archbishop of Westminster, was present at the devotions on 15 August 1946, and imparted Benediction to a large congregation. In October 1954, Cardinal McIntyre, Archbishop of Los Angeles, visited the Shrine. On 21 May 1955, on the occasion of the fiftieth anniversary of his Ordination, Most Rev. Dr Levame, Apostolic Nuncio to Ireland, visited Knock, and celebrated Mass at the Shrine altar there.

The development of pilgrimages since 1929 has been remarkable. To mark the Golden Jubilee of the Apparition in 1929 St Michan's Conference of the St Vincent de Paul Society in Dublin organised a special pilgrimage to Knock on the Sunday within the Octave of the Assumption, and this St Michan's pilgrimage became an annual event after 1929.

Pilgrimages were soon organised on a diocesan basis. Others were organised by the Children of Mary, Legion of Mary, Sacred Heart Sodalities and other bodies. After some years there was an organised pilgrimage on almost every Sunday from May to October. During the war years transport difficulties prevented many from coming, but pilgrimages of special significance during that time were the national Pilgrimage for Peace and the Protection of Ireland, 1 August 1940; the Children's Peace Pilgrimage, September 1940; the national Pilgrimage of Thanksgiving, 19 August 1945. After the war years, with the resumption of transport facilities, the crowds thronging Knock became larger than ever.

The climax was reached during the Marian Year, which was an outstanding year in the history of the Shrine. The year was solemnly opened at Knock on 8 December 1953, with solemn High Mass at which His Grace the Archbishop presided. The stream of pilgrims started immediately. Individual pilgrims and small groups were coming every day during the whole year, and it was estimated that about 1,000 pilgrims visited the Shrine every week day during the summer months. The first organised pilgrimage came on the 25 March under the auspices of the Tuam Legion of Mary. There was an organised pilgrimage on every Sunday from April to the end of October and some week days as well.

Certain days were of special significance. On 19 September 1954 the Pioneer Total Abstinence Pilgrimage proved to be the largest pilgrimage so far to assemble at Knock. It was estimated that about 50,000 people were present for the ceremonies. A pilgrimage of 2,000 officers and men of the National Army, under the leadership of the Chief of Staff and accompanied by the Army Chaplains, came on 26 September. The procession in the afternoon was headed by a colour party; the Statue of Our Lady of Knock was carried by officers and escorted by a guard of honour of officers. At the end of the Rosary the new Army Salute to Our Lady was given by the Army Band. It was a most spectacular and impressive day at Knock.

On the Feast of All Saints, Knock Shrine came before the notice of the whole Catholic world. On that day the Holy Father, Pope Pius XII, solemnly crowned the picture of Our Lady – *'Salus Populi Romani'* – in St Peter's Basilica in Rome. Over four hundred Marian Shrines in various parts of the world were represented at the ceremony. Knock Shrine was represented by a delegation headed by the Archbishop of Tuam. The banners of twenty Shrines were presented to the Holy Father in St Peter's, and each received from his hand a gold commemorative medal. The Knock Shrine banner was one of the twenty thus specially honoured.

For the closing of the Marian year in Knock two retreats – one for men, the other for women – were arranged by Fr Malone, Administrator, for the days preceding the Feast of the Immaculate Conception. The closing day itself was of historic significance. The Archbishop had obtained permission from the Vatican Chapter for the Coronation of the Statue of Our Lady of Knock on 8 December according to the ceremonial used by the Holy Father when crowning the picture, *'Salus Populi Romani'.* The weather conditions in Ireland on 8 December prevented many thousands from travelling. The church was nevertheless filled, and there was an overflow congregation who braved the sleet and snow in the church grounds. The solemn impressive ceremony of the crowning of the statue of Our Lady of Knock performed by the Archbishop was a fitting end to a year of continuous and intense devotion to Our Lady at her Shrine in Knock.

Developments of importance since 1954, and worthy of mention, are the conducting of retreats for lay people in St Mary's Hostel and the celebration of evening Mass at the Shrine altar on all Sundays and Holydays and all Thursdays during the period from May to October.

15.

The Knock Devotion

The development of the Knock devotion is itself a remarkable phenomenon. From the first great surge of pilgrims in the early years down to the present time the continuity of devotion and piety at Knock has remained unbroken. What is called the Station of Knock was a formula of prayer spontaneously adopted by the pilgrims themselves. All who came on pilgrimage prayed both inside and outside the church. The practice of reciting the Rosary whilst walking round the church outside was well established within six months after the apparition. The performing of the Stations of the Cross was soon added. This practice was certainly well established by 1895. For the big feastdays pilgrims were anxious to observe all-night vigils and to go to Confession and to receive Holy Communion. Some pilgrims added rigorous penances such as walking barefoot all the way to Knock and doing the 'rounds' of the church on their knees.

Ever since 1879 Knock always has been, and is now more than ever, a great centre of prayer. All through the pilgrimage season a continuous stream of prayers is ascending to heaven. It can be truly said that Knock is a spiritual power plant for the whole country. On what is called the quiet week day the devotion is not less edifying than on the big pilgrimage day. Every day the chorus of prayer continues from early morning till late at night. Inside the church there is silent prayer; outside the Rosary is being recited silently or aloud by individuals or by small groups. Talking of the Knock devotion in a sermon delivered at Knock in 1950, Very Rev. Paul Waldron, SSC, spoke as follows:[1]

'Knock is a shrine of prayer and a school of suffering. It is Mary's own hospital for her afflicted children. Here they come in their thousands, year after year to speak with Our Blessed Mother in consoling, intimate prayer, and to lay before her their poor bruised hearts and aching bodies. Some may be given the joy of health restored, but all are assured of a still greater blessing. They leave with the grace of a new understanding of their life and of the place that the cross has in making them like their suffering Saviour. They leave, formed after Mary's own Immaculate Heart ...

'We cherish the hope that Mary will continue to manifest more and more her great power at this Shrine, and that she will give a gracious answer to the prayer of the children who come here to honour her and seek her intercession.

'It was by prayer that Knock has become what it is today. It is by prayer that, please God, Knock will become still greater in the years to come. We piously believe that the Blessed Mother of God sanctified this ground by her visible presence over seventy years ago. And we believe that she continues to bless it by her presence, which, though no longer visible, is not less powerful or merciful. We believe that it is her wish that her children come here on pilgrimages and pray in procession and in private and that she will show a Mother's tender love, and manifest her Mother's power. And for this belief we have the testimony of credible witnesses. But we have another mighty foundation for our faith, the unshaken confidence of our Irish people in this Shrine of Knock. For nearly three quarters of a century, through fair weather and through foul, they have come in their thousands, and have made a path to this humble church. Every inch of this chapel yard has been sanctified by the footsteps of men and women who are high in heaven today. And many of them are there because of the sacrifices they made to honour Mary, and because of the graces they received within the hallowed walls of this Shrine. You may be sure that long line of Ireland's hidden saints, who tramped the roads of Ireland to Knock, wet and weary and hungry and footsore, in those dark days of our country, are looking down on you in the Beatific Vision. You can count on them to help you. But they in turn look to you to hold high the torch which Mary kindled on this hill, and which they took from her blessed hands, and kept burning down the years and have handed on to you. We must keep faith with those great souls, the pilgrims of the past. Pray, then, pray the Rosary especially, that the true pilgrim spirit may abide here in our day and in the generations to come. Mary will bless Knock in proportion as we try to be worthy of her blessing. Pray that each pilgrim who comes may experience Mary's presence and Mary's power, and may leave with that peace and joy of heart which Mary always obtains for her clients.

'Here you have a Shrine that has been built not with material stones, but with gems far more precious, the millions of Rosaries that loving hearts and worn fingers have laid all these years at the feet of Our Lady of Knock.'

On the day of an organised pilgrimage there are public devotions. A procession is formed and the Statue of Our Lady of Knock heads the procession. The ceremonies are carried out with simplicity and decorum without ostentation. Describing a pilgrimage scene at Knock in 1940, Very Rev. Canon Power of Birmingham stated for *The Standard*:

'I have seen religious ceremonies and processions in every part of the world. I have seen the Eucharistic Congress at Algiers, Dublin, Buenos Aires, Manilla – all magnificently carried out with regularity and rubrical beauty difficult to describe. But at Knock, whilst this was not entirely absent, there was something greater and deeper than all this external conformity. There was a sincerity, a depth of faith, which only Ireland can give to the world. Kneeling there upon Sunday morning during that High Mass, my thoughts went out to the great cathedrals, churches, colleges, Catholic schools and seminaries, convents and religious houses, to the ecclesiastical power houses in every country of the earth, which have been founded and kept going by the priest-sons of Ireland.

Here, in this tiny village on a Mayo hillside, I was at the very source of that almighty power which has spread the name of Jesus Christ throughout the English speaking world today. The nearest thing to Knock that I know in Europe is the village simplicity of Ars or the unspoilt rural beauty of Paray-de-Monial. Beyond all this I felt that Our Lady, in selecting Knock to reveal herself to her Irish children, must have felt very close to her own village home in Nazareth.'[2]

In a recent homily in the Basilica, the parish priest of Knock, Monsignor Joseph Quinn, spoke about Knock as a unique place of prayer and devotion:

'In the past half century Knock has seen extraordinary growth and development as a special place of pilgrimage and prayer – a place of evangelisation, devotion and spirituality. In its silence the Knock apparition speaks eloquently about the truths of our faith. The annual National Solemn Novena in August has been a great medium of evangelisation and memorable celebration of faith over the years. There is a hunger within us all for the transcendent, the divine. Today, many people are searching for ways to reach out to God and to connect with him. Sometimes they are not sure how best to do this. Knock Shrine can facilitate people in that search – and offers many opportunities for prayer and worship, for stillness and peace in our souls – so necessary amidst the noise, din, clutter and stress of modern life. Knock can help people experience peace, freedom, reconciliation and healing.

'The one hundred acres of the Shrine domain with its tasteful landscaped grounds of lawns, trees, shrubs, pathways and flowers speaks in itself of the wonder, beauty and majesty of the Creator God and helps us raise our hearts and minds to that God. Walking the pathways and processional routes at Knock is a vivid reminder that life is a pilgrim journey. There is the Liturgy at Knock – the summit of the Church's activity and the source of her vitality – the Masses, Ceremonies, Anointings, Rosaries, Processions. There's the Knock Holy Water. The Apparition Chapel, with its pristine white marble tableau of the apparition itself, is a haven of peace and a source of wonder and renewal for the tired and weary pilgrim. The

Confession Chapel provides an opportunity to celebrate the Sacrament of Reconciliation and experience God's forgiveness, healing and peace. There are many books in the Shrine Book Centre when "faith seeks understanding" and prayer needs support and nourishment, as it does. The museum reminds us of our heritage and roots. To lose your sense of history and heritage is to quickly lose your identity. In the Prayer Guidance Centre, trained prayer guides teach people how to pray with scripture. The Family Life Centre provides resources and support for the family. There's the Counselling Service at the Reconciliation Chapel. In the Blessed Sacrament Chapel one can spend a few moments with the Lord in prayer and adoration.

'There is the majestic Basilica of Our Lady, Queen of Ireland and the old parish church of St John the Baptist, recently refurbished.

'At Knock there is the Shrine staff and hundreds of volunteers, generous with their time, loyal, committed, friendly and helpful. At Knock there is a warm welcome for people of all faiths and none and for people of every race and culture.

'Above all there is Mary, the ever loving and caring Mother of the Incarnate Word, Jesus Christ, who invites us to do whatever her Son tells us – Mary, who with St Joseph, St John the Evangelist, the Lamb of God and the Angels, made Knock a sacred place, a place where Heaven and Earth meet, by their appearance and visitation here in 1879. Ever since, Knock is a unique place of pilgrimage, prayer, devotion and spirituality for countless members of God's pilgrim people.

'At Knock you can experience the powerful effect of witness and example. You see pilgrims of all ages pour out their hearts in prayer and open their hearts to God's peace, healing, reconciliation and divine life in the Eucharist and the Sacraments. You see people venerate the original stones from the Apparition Gable with reverence, respect and emotion. When you see the handmaids, stewards and other volunteers at their tasks, you experience care, love, faith and goodness the likes of which you rarely see – you experience the values of the Gospel in action. At Knock, as a philosopher once said, "the heart has reasons that reason knows nothing of". This is the core of Knock's spirituality.

'The sick, the disabled, the elderly who come to Knock – who are so much part of Knock – their faith, courage and endurance; their gratitude, their prayers and their tears can only touch and enrich you. They give every Mass we celebrate with them, and every ceremony in which they are involved a new meaning. The words of consecration – my body given for you/my blood poured out for you – have a new relevance. This too is at the heart of Knock's devotion and spirituality.

'St Therese, the Little Flower once wrote of prayer: "It's a surge of the heart; it's a simple look towards Heaven; it's a cry of recognition and love, embracing both trial and joy." This is what happens at Knock – every day. In the words of Jesus to his enquiring follower – "Come and see".'

For further information on Devotion at Knock, the reader is referred to Note 3, Chapter 15, in the Notes section at the end of the book. For further information on the history of Knock Shrine, the reader is referred to Note 4, Chapter 15, in the Notes section.

The reader is also referred to the following: *Reflecting at Knock* by Thomas Lane, CM, Columba, 2007; *Places Apart, Knock* by Eileen Good, Veritas, 2002.

16.

The Scriptural Meaning of the Apparition

We know from scripture that God prepared his people during many centuries for the coming of the Messias by sending prophets to reveal gradually God's eternal plan of salvation. In a similar, but proportionately lesser way, God provided, in advance, signs that showed the way to passages in the Bible that help to explain the images in the apparition.

The Signs

There are four signs emanating from the new church in Knock:

1. John the Baptist, Precursor of the Messias, Patron Saint of Knock church. He introduced Jesus to the people, proclaiming, 'Behold, the Lamb of God who takes away the sin of the world'. The Lamb of God was God's own Son who was led like a lamb to the slaughter and who offered himself in sacrifice on a cross for the salvation of the world. These words of John the Baptist were prophetic.

2. The first inscription on the stone tablet inserted into the west gable wall of the church is taken from Psalm 118 (117); it reads: 'This is the gate of the Lord; the just shall enter into it.' This psalm was sung on the annual festival day of the sacrifice of the Lamb of the Passover in the Temple of Jerusalem. The Lamb of the Passover prefigured Jesus Christ, the Lamb of God.

3. The second inscription on the stone tablet reads: 'My House

shall be called the house of prayer to all nations.' These are the words of Jesus, the true Lamb of God, which he spoke in the Temple of Jerusalem, and which led to the process that within a few days resulted in his death on the cross.

4. The place chosen for the apparition was the parish church in Knock. Catholic churches are prefigured by the Tabernacle in the desert and the Temple in Jerusalem. Each church has an altar on which the sacrifice of the Lamb of God is perpetuated in the celebration of the Eucharist. Near the altar is a tabernacle where Jesus Christ is really, truly and substantially present in the Blessed Sacrament of the Eucharist. The altar and tabernacle of Knock church were situated at the inner middle of the south gable wall; at the outer middle of the wall the images of the Lamb, altar and cross were seen; the outer gable wall of the church was part of the apparition scene.

The Meaning of a Unique Apparition

The meaning of the apparition is communicated by the images of the apparition itself and by the signs given when the church was built in 1828. The images and signs highlight passages in the Old and New Testaments which explain the meaning of the apparition; the passages highlighted in scripture reveal God's plan of salvation for the world.

Images, Signs, Symbols

No words were spoken in the apparition; communication was made by biblical images which were familiar to ordinary Christian people; the positions of the images, the bodily posture, the attitude of each image, the relative positions of the images – all these silent symbols are as eloquent as words, written or spoken. Religious icons, sculptures, paintings, stained glass, are all art forms used in churches throughout the centuries, as means of instruction on the life of our Lord, the Mother of Jesus, and other religious themes.

The Knock Apparition – Similar, but Different

The apparition at Knock is similar in some ways to religious art forms, but essentially it is different. It appeared suddenly without explanation and remained visible for over two hours during some day light time and some night time surrounded by a brilliant light; the images were not composed of any material substance; they were visible to the human eye, but could not be felt by touch. When a witness tried to embrace the feet of our Lady, she found nothing in her embrace. The apparition disappeared as suddenly as it appeared.

An International Language

The images, signs and symbols deliver a message from the Bible that is understood by peoples of all nations and languages. Without words they speak an international language. In a sense the effect resembles the preaching of the apostles on the first Pentecost; their audience came from all known nations; yet each of them heard the apostles speaking in their own language.

The Character of the Apparition

The apparition is regular, reasonable and harmonious in design; it portrays dignity, goodness and holiness; one of the witnesses described it as 'miraculous lights' and 'beautiful visions'; all the witnesses believed that the images they saw were from heaven. The apparition itself, as described by the witnesses, bears its own stamp of authenticity. The design of the apparition tableau expresses the most profound truths in God's plan of salvation. Knowledge of God's plan of salvation presupposes an understanding of sacred scripture and theology beyond the knowledge of the witnesses. The witnesses could not have designed or invented the apparition. The character of the apparition is the seal of its origin. It could not have been produced by natural causes.

An additional important detail is that, though there was heavy rain all through the time of the apparition, no rain fell on the images or on the ground beneath them. This detail was a sign of heavenly intervention.

Other Signs of Divine Origin

In the years following the apparition numerous cures were claimed by pilgrims. It is not likely that all these cures were miraculous. But many cures were so remarkable that one could believe they could not be due to natural causes alone. In these cases the pilgrims claimed that their cures came from their prayers at Knock Shrine, or that they came from the use of cement from the apparition gable wall. Such cures would be a sign of divine origin.

An outstanding development at Knock Shrine is the continuous and increasing spiritual devotion practised there. Ever since 1879 Knock has been, and is now more than ever, a powerful centre of prayer and of the reception of the sacraments of Reconciliation and the Blessed Eucharist. Knock is a source of scriptural spirituality not only for Ireland but for pilgrims from other countries worldwide. This beneficial result from the apparition is a further sign of its divine origin.

For the findings of an inquiry into the origin of the apparition at Knock, the reader is referred to page 98, Chapter 8.

The Two Panels

The apparition has often been described as a tableau with two panels; the first consists of the Lamb standing on an altar with a cross behind it; the second panel has three images, those of the Blessed Virgin Mary, St Joseph and St John the Evangelist.

The First Panel

The panel of the Lamb encapsulates the sacrifice of Jesus Christ, the Lamb of God, on the cross and the perpetuation of that sacrifice in the Eucharist on an altar until the end of time. The standing position of the Lamb, Jesus Christ, means he is alive; he has risen from the dead after his sacrifice on the cross. Jesus Christ is the true Lamb of God who takes away the sin of the world. By his death on the cross and his resurrection he redeems the world.

In the Book of Revelation St John describes part of the heavenly liturgy: 'I saw a Lamb standing, as though it had been slain. All the angels and saints were worshipping the Lamb saying, "Worthy is the Lamb who was slain, to receive power and wealth and wisdom and might and honour and glory and blessing".' (Rev 5:12)

The Second Panel – The Three Images

The panel of the three images was on a lower level than the panel of the Lamb, but in relation to the whole tableau it was the panel that attracted most attention from the witnesses. The panel of the Lamb was in the central position of the gable wall, but in relation to the other panel it was slightly in the background. The central image of the three was that of the Blessed Virgin Mary; it was on a slightly higher level than the other two; on the right of the Blessed Virgin was her husband, St Joseph; on her left was St John the Evangelist. The image of the Blessed Virgin Mary formed the focal point for the whole apparition. One of the witnesses said, she 'was so taken with the Blessed Virgin' that she did not pay attention to any other.

The central image is described, in part, by witnesses. The Virgin stood erect with 'eyes raised to heaven, her hands elevated to the shoulders ... she wore a large white cloak ... she wore a crown on her head – rather a large crown'. Other witnesses said she 'appeared to be praying, she was in the attitude of prayer'. The descriptions given of the Blessed Virgin in the apparition are similar to the description given of her in the Book of Revelation: 'And a great portent appeared in heaven, a woman clothed with the sun, with the moon under her feet, and on her head a crown of twelve stars.' (Rev 12:1-2)

The Central Message of the Apparition

In heaven Mary, as Queen of Heaven and Earth, leads all the angels and saints in the heavenly liturgy, giving adoration, thanks and praise to God, Father, Son and Holy Spirit. In the apparition Mary, as Queen and Mother of the Church, leads all the faithful in the earthly liturgy, the celebration of the Eucharist, in giving adoration, thanks and praise to God, Father, Son and Holy Spirit. She has her eyes turned towards heaven; beside her is the panel of the Eucharist;

on the inner side of the gable wall are the altar and tabernacle of the church building. By her upturned eyes Mary is uniting the two liturgies, the earthly and the heavenly, because they are essentially the same liturgy; the earthly is heaven on earth.[1] Mary, the Mother of Jesus, and the Mother of his Church, is the model of eucharistic adoration; she is a woman of the Eurcharist.[2] Our Lady of Knock is Our Lady of the Eucharist.

St Joseph

St Joseph was a holy man chosen by God to be the husband of Mary and the foster father of Jesus. His saintliness was inspired by the spirituality of the Old Testament. In time of danger he was the Protector of the Child Jesus and his Mother. He supported the Holy Family by his work as a carpenter. In 1870 Pope Pius IX named him Patron of the Universal Church. In the apparition St Joseph stood at the right of the Blessed Virgin. 'In the figure of St Joseph the head was slightly bent, and inclined toward the Blessed Virgin, as if paying her respect'; 'His hands were joined like a person at prayer.' St Joseph was expressing his respect for his beloved Spouse, the Virgin Mary. He had his hands joined in prayer; by this sign he was worshipping the Lamb of God, and praying for the Church.

St John the Evangelist

St John the Evangelist was at first a disciple of John the Baptist. He and Andrew, the brother of Peter, heard John the Baptist introducing Jesus to the crowd saying, 'Behold the Lamb of God'. The two disciples followed Jesus to the place where he was staying, and they stayed with him that day. Later they both became disciples of Jesus. John was the only apostle who followed Jesus to Calvary, and stood with Mary at the foot of the cross, when Jesus, the Lamb of God, offered himself in sacrifice on the cross to take away the sin of the world. He heard the words spoken by Jesus to his Mother, 'Woman, behold, your son', and the words spoken by Jesus to John himself, 'Behold, your Mother'. John had already been the beloved disciple of the Lord; now, by these words Jesus made John an adopted member of the Holy Family. In his Gospel John records the instruction on the Eucharist given by Jesus in Capernaum. He wrote the Book of Revelation in which he describes a vision he had of heaven, where he saw the heavenly celebration of the Eucharist.

In the apparition, John, wearing the liturgical vestments of a bishop, is seen preaching; he is drawing attention both to the sacrifice of the Lamb of God and to Mary the Mother of Jesus; he is emphasising the redeeming sacrifice of the Lamb and the singular and unique role of the Mother of Jesus in her participation in the sacrifice of her Son.

The Central Mystery of God's Plan of Salvation

The images and signs of the Knock apparition highlight the passages in scripture that reveal God's plan of salvation for the world. Identifying and examining those passages would require a full book for themselves. Here we will concentrate on the central mystery of God's plan, that is, the sacrifice of God the Father's own Son, the Lamb of God, the Redeemer. The sacrifice of our redemption is the sacrifice of Jesus Christ on the cross and the perpetuation of that sacrifice in the Eucharist. In the following pages we will meditate on those scriptural passages that highlight the sacrifice of Jesus Christ on the cross and the perpetuation of that sacrifice in the Eucharist.

17.

The Blessed Eucharist

SCRIPTURAL PREFIGURATIONS OF THE PASSION AND DEATH OF JESUS CHRIST AND THE EUCHARIST

The Sacrifice of Abel

For his offering to God, Abel picked out from the 'firstlings of his flock' a lamb. The Lord was pleased with the offering of Abel.

The Sacrifice of Abraham

To test the fidelity of Abraham, God commanded him to sacrifice his only son, Isaac, whom he loved. In obedience to God's command, Abraham made all necessary arrangements for the sacrifice of his son on the top of a mountain. Isaac, in obedience to his father, carried the wood for his own sacrifice to the top of the mountain. When they came to the place for the sacrifice, Isaac asked his father, 'Where is the lamb for a burnt offering?' Abraham answered, 'God will provide [for] himself the lamb for a burnt offering, my son'. This reply of Abraham was prophetic. The Lamb that God provided for sacrifice was his own divine Son, whom he loved, and who willingly offered himself in sacrifice for the salvation of the world.

When Abraham was about to sacrifice his son, God called to him from heaven and told him not to lay his hand on the lad or to do anything to him, 'for now I know that you fear God, seeing that you have not withheld your son, your only son, from me'. Abraham looked around him and saw a ram caught in a thicket by his horns; he took the ram and 'offered it up as a burnt offering instead of his son'. God was pleased with Abraham's obedience and said to him, 'I will bless you indeed, and I will multiply your descendants as the stars in heaven, and as the sand which is on the seashore' (Gen 22).

This episode prefigures the Passion and Death of Jesus Christ. It also reveals the love of God the Father for his people. Jesus says of his Father, 'God so loved the world that he gave his only Son that whoever believes in him should not perish but have eternal life' (Jn 3:16).

The Sacrifice of Melchizedek

Melchizedek was King of Salem and Priest of the Most High God. He offered a sacrifice of bread and wine in thanksgiving for victories gained by Abraham over his enemies. He blessed Abraham and said, 'Blessed be Abraham by God Most High, maker of heaven and earth; and blessed be God Most High, who has delivered your enemies into your hand' (Gen 14:18-20).

Melchizedek was both Priest and King. His priesthood was unique in the Old Testament; it was not inherited; there was no mention of father or mother or of any other relatives. It was without beginning or end. His priesthood prefigured the priesthood of Jesus Christ. His sacrifice of bread and wine prefigured the sacrifice of Jesus on the cross, which would be perpetuated in the Eucharist under the appearances of bread and wine.

These signs reveal that from the beginning God the Father had decreed in his divine plan of salvation that the sacrifice of his Divine Son on the cross would be perpetuated in an unbloody manner in all nations until the end of time, under the appearances of bread and wine.

The Messias – The Son of God

In Psalm 110 the author, King David, says in praise of the Messias, 'The Lord says to my Lord, "Sit at my right hand, till I make your enemies your footstool"'. To 'sit at God's right hand' means that God will share his power and authority with the Messias King. In scripture, to sit at God's right hand is a prerogative given exclusively to God's own Son.

The psalmist also says: 'The Lord has sworn an oath he will not change. "You are a priest for ever, a priest like Mechizedek of old".' The Messias will be an eternal priest; he will offer an eternal sacrifice under the appearances of bread and wine.

The Sacrifice of the Lamb of the Passover

The sacrifice of the lamb of the Passover was a new sacrifice instituted by God for the liberation of the Israelite people from slavery in Egypt. The blood of the sacrificed lamb was sprinkled on the doorposts and lintels of the Israelite houses to save their first-borns from death. The flesh of the sacrificed lamb was eaten with unleavened bread and bitter herbs. This sacrifice prefigured the sacrifice of Jesus on the cross which he offered for the liberation of all peoples from the slavery of sin.

The Feast of the Pasch

God commanded the people to celebrate the sacrifice of the first passover lamb each year on the exact anniversary day from generation to generation. The annual celebration was called the Feast of the Pasch. It was more than a recalling to memory of the events; it was a making present again of the rite of the first passover with all its principal parts. At the Paschal meal the roasted lamb was eaten along with unleavened bread and a cup of wine. For the people of Israel the Feast of the Pasch was the same passover sacrifice being celebrated each year. The feast of the Pasch prefigured the Eucharist which would be celebrated on every day of the year forever. For Jesus and his followers the last celebration of the Jewish Pasch took place at the Last Supper, when Jesus instituted the sacrifice and sacrament of the Eucharist.

The Unleavened Bread

Originally the offering of unleavened bread had its own separate ceremony. Later it was offered along with the rite of the offering of the passover lamb, and came to have the same meaning as the passover. It prefigured the unleavened bread over which Jesus pronounced the words, 'This is my body'.

The Suffering Servant of God in Isaias

The prophet Isaias describes the life of a perfect servant of God, who lives a life of suffering, which he offers to God to atone for the sins of the people. This servant of God foreshadows Jesus in his Passion and Death. The following extracts are from Isaias:

> He was despised and rejected by men,
> a man of sorrows, and acquainted with grief;
> he was wounded for our transgressions,
> he was bruised for our iniquities.
> The Lord has laid upon him the iniquity of us all.
> He was oppressed, and he was afflicted.
> Yet he opened not his mouth; like a lamb that is led to the slaughter,
> and like a sheep that before its shearers is dumb,
> so he opened not his mouth.
> (Isa 53:3-7)

The prophecy of Isaias shows that the Messias will not be a political king; his kingdom will not be of this world. By his sufferings he will atone for the sins of his people.

The Suffering Disciple in Psalm 22 also prefigures Jesus in his Passion. The first verse of this psalm is a fervent prayer to God for help. Some of the verses resemble prophecies which were literally fulfilled when Jesus was crucified. On the cross Jesus, trusting in his heavenly Father, uttered the first verse of this psalm: 'My God, My God, why hast thou forsaken me?'

The psalm has two parts; the first describes the sufferings of the psalmist:

My God, my God, why hast thou forsaken me?
Why are thou so far from helping me, from the words of my groaning?
O My God, I cry by day, but thou dost not answer;
and by night, but find no rest.
Yet thou art holy, enthroned on the praises of Israel.
In thee our fathers trusted;
they trusted, and thou didst deliver them.
But I am a worm and no man;
scorned by men, and despised by the people.
All who see me mock at me, they wag their heads;
he committed his cause to the Lord; let him deliver him,
let him rescue him, for he delights in him.
My strength is dried up like a potsherd,
and my tongue cleaves to my jaws;
thou dost lay me in the dust of death,
a company of evildoers encircle me;
They have pierced my hands and my feet, I can count all my bones;
they stare and gloat over me; they divide my garments among them,
and for my raiment they cast lots.
(Ps 22:1-8, 15-18)

In the second part of the psalm the psalmist expresses his confidence in God that he will answer his prayers, and he vows to give him praise:

You who fear the Lord, praise him! All you sons of Jacob glorify him,
and stand in awe of him, all you sons of Israel!
For he has not despised or abhorred the affliction of the afflicted,
and he has not hid his face from him,
but has heard, when he cried to him.
From thee comes my praise in the great congregation;
my vows I will pay before those who fear him.
(Ps 22:23-25)

In this psalm the psalmist prefigures Jesus in his Passion.

The Manna in the Desert

The manna was the bread which the Lord gave to his people during the forty years when they were journeying in the desert. It was called the bread from heaven. Jesus told the people that his father gives the true bread from heaven. 'For the bread of God is that which comes down from heaven and gives life to the world.' (Ex 16:14ff; Jn 6:32-33) The manna in the desert prefigures the Eucharist.

The Miracle of the Loaves and Fishes

The first event recorded in chapter six of St John's Gospel is the multiplication of the five barley loaves and two fish. 'Jesus took the loaves, and when had given thanks, he distributed them to those who were seated; so also the fish, as much as they wanted.' (Jn 6:1-11) When the people saw the miracle performed by Jesus, they believed that he was the prophet who was to come, and they wanted to make him king.

Jesus performed this miracle because he had compassion on the people who were hungry. But as happened on other occasions, he had a deeper purpose in mind. He wanted to prepare the minds of the people for the announcement he would make that he would give them a more wonderful bread, the bread that had come down from heaven. In chapter five of St John's Gospel, Jesus tries to get the people to make an act of faith in him that he has the authority and power from God the Father to do what he promises to do: 'The works which the Father has granted me to accomplish, these very works, which I am doing, bear me witness that the Father has sent me.' (Jn 5:36) The miracle of the loaves was performed by Jesus through his power and authority as the only Son of the Father.

The Significance of the Miracle of the Loaves

The miracle of feeding five thousand people with a small amount of food and having more food left over than he had at the beginning is a sign of his power to feed an innumerable number of people with his Body and Blood without any diminution in his Risen and Glorified Body. The gathering up of the fragments left over, lest they be lost, symbolises the worship due to consecrated hosts left over after the celebration of the Eucharist.

Jesus promises the Blessed Eucharist

The miracle of the loaves is directly connected with the discourse which Jesus gave on the Bread of Life in the synagogue at Capernaum. The people were so amazed at the amount of food that he had provided for them that they followed him to Capernaum. Jesus spoke to them in a dialogue on the meaning of the Bread of Life. He said to them, 'Truly, truly, I say to you, you seek me, not because you saw the signs, but because you ate your fill of the loaves. Do not labour for the food which perishes, but for the food which endures to eternal life, which the Son of Man will give you; for on him God the Father has set his seal' (Jn 6:26-27).

Jesus is about to reveal to them the mystery of the Blessed Eucharist. He wants them to believe that he has the authority and power from God the Father to do what he promises.

The Bread which I shall give is my Flesh

Jesus continues his discourse: 'Truly, I say to you, he who believes has eternal life. Your fathers ate the manna in the wilderness, and they died. This is the bread which comes down from heaven, that a man may eat of it and not die. I am the living bread which came down from heaven; if any one eats of this bread, he will live for ever; and the bread which I shall give for the life of the world is my flesh.' (Jn 6:47-51)

The Jews heard these words; they understood them in their literal sense; they disputed among themselves, and said, 'How can this man give us his flesh to eat?' Jesus said to them:

> 'Truly, truly, I say to you,
> **unless you eat the flesh of the Son of Man and drink his**

blood you have no life in you;
he who eats my flesh and drinks my blood has eternal life,
and I will raise him up on the last day.
For **my flesh is food indeed, and my blood is drink indeed.**
He who eats my flesh and drinks my blood abides in me and
I in him.

As the living Father sent me, and I live because of the
Father, so he who eats me will live because of me. This is the
bread which came down from heaven, not such as the fathers
ate and died; he who eats this bread will live for ever.' This he
said in the synagogue, as he taught in Capernaum.
(Jn 6:52-59)

Some who did not believe

The Jews understood the words of Jesus in the literal sense; they did
not believe. If Jesus had meant his words to be understood in a
figurative, or symbolic or metaphorical sense, he would have told
the people that his words were not to be taken literally. That would
have been the practice of Jewish teachers of religion at that time.
Jesus did not withdraw one word of the statement he had made.
Instead, he made another statement, emphasising, repeating and
confirming his words about eating his flesh and drinking his blood
in the literal sense of the words.

Many of Jesus' own disciples did not believe; they said, 'This is a
hard saying and who can listen to it?' Jesus said to them, 'Do you
take offence at this? Then what if you were to see the Son of Man
ascending where he was before? It is the spirit that gives life, the
flesh is of no avail; the words I have spoken to you are spirit and
life' (Jn 6:60-64).

Jesus was sent by the Father – He will return to the Father

Jesus recalls for his listeners that he was sent by the Father to do the
works that his Father gave him to do. They will be able to see him
ascending to heaven after he has completed these works.

Jesus says, 'It is the spirit that gives life, the flesh is of no avail'.

Human flesh of itself is of no avail; but the flesh of Jesus is unique; it is in union with his divine Person; Jesus made his flesh a source of life. 'It is the Spirit that gives life.'

Human understanding is of no avail for understanding the works of God; it is only the gifts of the Holy Spirit that enable human beings to make an act of faith in the word of God. A crude, cannibalistic understanding of eating the flesh and drinking the blood is all that human understanding can achieve. With the help of the Holy Spirit, the true, literal, supernatural meaning of eating the flesh and drinking the blood is accepted in faith.

The unbelief of people on two occasions mentioned in St John's Gospel was due to their lack of faith in Jesus Christ, lack of faith in God. The supernatural act of faith is the act 'whereby, inspired and assisted by the grace of God, we believe that the things which he has revealed are true; not because of the intrinsic truth of the things, viewed by the natural light of reason, but because of the authority of God himself who reveals them, and who can neither be deceived nor deceive' (Vatican I, *Dei Filius*, Chapter 3).

Peter, Head of the Apostles, Professes his Faith in Jesus

After this, many of the disciples of Jesus went away and no longer followed him. Jesus said to the apostles, 'Will you also, go away?' This question put by Jesus to his apostles shows that faith in the Eucharist is essential for his followers. He is prepared to let even his apostles go, if they do not believe his teaching on the Eucharist. Simon Peter answered, 'Lord, to whom shall we go? You have the words of eternal life; and we have believed, and have come to know that you are the Holy One of God' (Jn 6:67-69). This profession of faith by Peter is an example for all followers of Jesus Christ.

At the Last Supper Jesus fulfilled his promise to give his flesh to eat and his blood to drink.

The Last Journey of Jesus to Jerusalem

The cleansing of the Temple took place at the end of the last journey travelled by Jesus to Jerusalem. On the road, starting from

Galilee, Jesus continued to teach the people, and to give special instructions to his apostles. On three separate occasions he foretold to his apostles his Passion, Death and Resurrection. By announcing his sufferings in advance to his chosen twelve he showed his eagerness to fulfil the will of his Father as revealed in the scriptures. While he called himself the Son of Man, he knew he was the Messias, the Son of the Father, sent by the Father to redeem the world. He did not want to declare publicly that he was the Messias, until he had come to the end of his journey in Jerusalem.

The Third Announcement by Jesus of His Passion, Death and Resurrection

As they were coming nearer to Jerusalem, the end of their journey, Jesus took the apostles aside again, and spoke to them the third time about his Passion: 'Behold, we are going up to Jerusalem; and the Son of Man will be delivered to the chief priests and the scribes and they will condemn him to death, and deliver him to the gentiles; and they will mock him, and spit upon him, and scourge him, and kill him; and after three days he will rise.' (Mk 10:33-34)

The Triumphal Entry of Jesus into Jerusalem

When Jesus and his apostles came to the boundary of Jerusalem, he made preparations for his entry into the city. Two of his disciples 'brought the colt to Jesus, and they threw their garments on it, and he sat upon it' (Mk 11:7). Jesus entered as the king of peace. He did not enter on a war horse but on a donkey, an animal used for peaceful purposes by ordinary people, the poor and the humble. When he entered the city, the ordinary people and the children received him as their Messias with great joy. They cried out, 'Hosanna! Blessed is he who comes in the name of the Lord. Blessed is the Kingdom of our father David that is coming! Hosanna in the highest!' (Mk 11:9-10).

Now Jesus accepts the declaration of the people that he is the Messias.

The Cleansing of the Temple

After the solemn entry of Jesus into Jerusalem, he went to the temple and looked around the whole building. He then went from the city to Bethany with his apostles. The following day he returned to the city, and again visited the temple. He drove out those who were buying and selling there, and those engaged in worldly business. He taught the people, and said to them, 'Is it not written, "My house shall be called the house of prayer for all the nations?" But you have made it a den of robbers' (Mk 11:17).

By the cleansing of the temple Jesus is asserting his divine authority in his father's house. The chief priests and the scribes heard about Jesus' entry into the city, and his cleansing of the temple, and his words spoken there. Because of all these things the authorities of the temple 'sought a way to destroy him' (Mk 11:18).

The Death of Jesus is sought

The next morning Jesus and his apostles returned to the city and visited the temple. When Jesus was walking inside, the chief priests and the scribes and the elders approached him, and said to him, 'By what authority are you doing these things or who gave you this authority to do them?' Jesus said to them, 'I will ask you a question; answer me, and I will tell you by what authority I do these things. Was the baptism of John from heaven or from men? Answer me' (Mk 11:28-30). The question from Jesus perplexed the Jewish authorities. They knew from the testimony given to them by John that Jesus was the Messias. If they were to say that John's baptism was from heaven, they will be asked why they did not believe in him. If they say that John's baptism was from men, they will fear the people, for all believed that John was a prophet. They answered, 'We do not know'. Jesus said to them, 'Neither will I tell you by what authority I do these things' (Mk 11:33).

After the cleansing, the disciples of Jesus remembered that it was written in a psalm, 'Zeal for thy house will consume me' (Ps 69:9). When the Jewish authorities asked him, 'What sign have you to show us for this?' Jesus answered, 'Destroy this temple, and in three days I will raise it up' (Jn 2:19). Jesus spoke of the temple of his body.

Judas offers to betray Jesus
Judas Iscariot, one of the chosen twelve, went to the chief priests and told them he was prepared to betray Jesus to them; they gave him thirty pieces of silver. Judas was then waiting for an opportunity to betray him.

The Passover
The sacrifice of the passover lamb took place in the temple the day before the celebration of the passover meal. The meal was held in the households on the night of 14–15 Nisan. It consisted in eating the roasted flesh of the sacrificed lamb along with unleavened bread and a cup of wine. This was the occasion chosen by Jesus for the institution of the Blessed Eucharist. The combined ceremony of the passover and the institution of the Eucharist is called the Last Supper.

The Last Supper – Preparations
'And on the first day of Unleavened Bread, when they sacrificed the passover lamb, his disciples said to him, "Where will you have us go and prepare for you to eat the Passover?"' Jesus had already chosen the venue, and had made arrangements with the householder for the celebration of the passover. He sent two of his disciples into the city, having given them directions to the place he had chosen. He told them, when they would arrive there, the householder would 'show them a large upper room furnished and ready. There prepare for us' (Mk 12:15). The disciples did as they were told; they prepared the passover.

The Betrayal by Judas
When the time came for the passover meal, Jesus sat at the table with the twelve apostles, and as they were eating, he said to them, 'Truly, I say to you, one of you will betray me'. The apostles were

grieved to hear this; they were wondering who it was who would betray their Master. They began to ask, 'Is it I, Lord?' He answered, 'He who has dipped his hand in the dish with me will betray me. The Son of Man goes as it is written of him, but woe to that man by whom the Son of Man is betrayed. It would have been better for that man, if he had not been born'. Judas, who betrayed him, said, 'Is it I, Master?' Jesus said to him, 'You have said so' (Mt 26:20-25).

* * *

THE INSTITUTION OF THE EUCHARIST

The institution of the Eucharist is reported in the Gospels of Matthew, Mark, Luke and in St Paul's First Letter to the Corinthians. All four accounts are substantially the same. Luke and Paul have some details not contained in Matthew or Mark. The four accounts provide a composite report on the institution of the Eucharist. In his Gospel John does not give a report on the institution itself. In the sixth chapter of his Gospel John gives the discourse on the Eucharist in which Jesus promises to give his flesh to eat and his blood to drink.

The Eucharistic Prayers of the Mass

In the four Eucharistic Prayers of the Mass the words of the Institution narrative are substantially the same, though varying slightly, but the words of Consecration are exactly the same in all four prayers. In Eucharistic Prayer I, the following is the text of the institution narrative and the Consecration:

> The day before he suffered he took bread in his sacred hands and looking up to heaven, to you, his almighty Father, he gave you thanks and praise.
> He broke the bread, gave it to his disciples, and said:
> **Take this, all of you, and eat it:**
> **this is my body which will be given up for you.**
> When supper was ended, he took the cup.

Again he gave you thanks and praise,
gave the cup to his disciples, and said:
Take this, all of you, and drink from it:
this is the cup of my blood,
the blood of the new and everlasting covenant.
It will be shed for you and for all
so that sins may be forgiven.
Do this in memory of me.
(The Roman Missal)

The New and Everlasting Covenant

In the Old Covenant of Mount Sinai God gave laws to his people Israel to be obeyed and observed by them. The obedience and observance to the laws established a holy relationship between God and his people. In return God would be their Protector and Helper in all their needs. If they did not obey, God would withdraw his protection from them. The Old Covenant was ratified by the offering of animals in sacrifice.

In the New Covenant the Church is the new People of God; the Covenant is the communion of God and his people. The Eucharist, the sacraments, the Gospel message are the new living relationship between God and his people, a relationship of love. The New Covenant was ratified by the blood of Jesus Christ, the Blood of the New and Everlasting Covenant. The Covenant will be perfected in Heaven (cf. *Catechism of the Catholic Church (CCC)*, pp. 2562–4, 2795).

The Last Supper – The Institution of the Eucharist

Jesus chose the Passover meal as the most meaningful occasion for the institution of the Eucharist. At the traditional Passover meal the roasted flesh of the sacrificed Passover Lamb was eaten along with unleavened bread and a cup of wine. It was in the course of this meal that Jesus instituted the Eucharist. In the Eucharist the Lamb was Jesus himself, the true Lamb of God, who offered himself in sacrifice to take away the sin of the world. The bread and wine for the Passover meal were changed by Jesus into his own Body and Blood. The words used by Jesus declared this changing; they also declared the simultaneous offering of himself in sacrifice. The separate consecrations into his Body and Blood reveal the separation of his Body and Blood in sacrifice. In the institution of the Eucharist Jesus anticipated his death on the cross on the following day and also his subsequent Resurrection. Jesus gives to his apostles his Body to eat and his Blood to drink. In the Bible the word 'body' means more than a merely physical body. It means the whole person, in whom body and spirit are one. In receiving Holy Communion the communicant receives Jesus Christ, Body and Blood, soul and divinity. The Body received is the Risen Body of Christ. In the institution of the Eucharist Jesus anticipated both his death on the cross and his Resurrection. The Eucharist and the Resurrection are joined. Jesus gives himself in Holy Communion under the appearance of food, that is, under the appearances of bread and wine.

The Words of Consecration

Jesus took bread, gave it to his disciples and said, 'Take this, all of you, and eat it: This is my Body which will be given up for you'. The words, 'This is my Body', are so simple, so clear and so emphatic, that they leave no scope for being interpreted as being a sign, a symbol, figure or metaphor. Only one meaning is reasonably possible, the literal meaning. To suggest that when Jesus said the words, 'This is my Body', he meant, 'This is a symbol of my Body', is doing violence to language. The words, 'which will be given up for you', mean that this body is being offered up in sacrifice 'for you and for all'. St Paul expresses the meaning this way: 'And being found in human form he humbled himself and became obedient unto death, even death on a cross.' (Phil 2:8)

When supper was ended, Jesus took a cup filled with wine and said, 'Take this, all of you, and drink from it: this is the cup of my Blood, the blood of the new and everlasting covenant. It will be shed for you and for all so that sins may be forgiven'.

By changing the wine into his blood, Jesus anticipated the sacrifice of himself on the cross which would take place on the following day in the outpouring of all his blood, his life, for the salvation of the world.

'Do this in memory of me.' This was a command given by Jesus to his apostles and their successors to do what he had just done, that is, in the celebration of the Eucharist he wanted to be remembered by the perpetuation, the making present, of the one sacrifice of himself which he offered on the cross. This one sacrifice is the eternal sacrifice of Jesus being made present perpetually through the ministry of the bishops and the priests of the Church in all the generations till the end of time. Through this perpetuation of his sacrifice on the cross Jesus made it possible for all successive generations to unite themselves with him, the Eternal High Priest, in his one eternal sacrifice. This perpetual sacrifice is called the sacrifice of the Eucharist, the sacrifice of the Mass. It is the gift of himself given to the Church by Jesus Christ, the divine gift of love for his people.

The Perpetuation of the Eternal Sacrifice
After the descent of the Holy Spirit, the apostles did as the Lord commanded them. They celebrated the Eucharist in the homes of the Christian people. They made present the sacrifice of Jesus Christ under the appearance of bread and wine. They gave the Body and Blood of the Lord to be consumed under the appearance of bread and wine. The name they gave to the Eucharist was the 'Breaking of Bread'. The apostles instructed their successors to celebrate the Eucharist. In his First Letter to the Corinthians, St Paul instructs his converts on the worthy reception of the Eucharist, and warns them against unworthy reception which would make them guilty of sacrilege 'against the Body and Blood of the Lord'.

For two thousand years the Catholic Church has faithfully carried out the Lord's command. The holy sacrifice of the Eucharist, or as it is also called, the holy sacrifice of the Mass, has been celebrated in an ever increasing number of places worldwide. The prophecy of Malachi has been fulfilled: 'For from the rising of the sun to its setting my name is great among the nations, and in every place incense is offered to my name, and a pure offering; for my name is great among the nations, says the Lord of hosts.' (Mal 1:11)

The Mystery of Faith

The Eucharist is a mystery; we cannot fully understand it. We believe in the Eucharist on the word of Jesus Christ. He explained carefully the meaning of the Eucharist; we believe the word of Jesus who speaks only what is true. We also believe in his power to do what he promises, even though we do not understand how it takes place.

About the Eucharist, St Ambrose wrote: 'Could not Christ's word, which can make from nothing, what did not exist, change existing things into what they were not before? It is no less a feat to give things their original nature than to change their nature.' (*CCC*, p. 1375)

Transubstantiation

Transubstantiation was a new word introduced about 1079 to describe the divine act by which Jesus Christ changes bread and wine into his Body and Blood. The word is composed of two Latin words, *trans* and *substantia*. The composite word describes accurately the act of changing one substance into another. It seems to have been introduced by the theologian, Hildebert of Tours. It was adapted by other contemporary Latin theologians, and by the subsequent General Councils – the Fourth Lateran Council (1215), the Council of Lyons (1274) and later by the Council of Trent (1545–1563).

The Literal Meaning of the Words

When Jesus spoke the words of consecration separately over the bread and wine, 'This is my Body' ... 'This is the cup of my Blood', the bread and the wine became separately, by the power of Jesus Christ, the true Body and Blood of Jesus. The total substance of the bread was changed into the Body of Christ, and the total substance of the wine was changed into the Blood of Christ Jesus. Christ is really, truly and substantially present in the Eucharist, body, blood, soul and divinity. We do not understand how this change takes place. We believe it on the word of Jesus Christ, who can neither be deceived nor deceive. The doctrine of the Real Presence of Jesus in the Eucharist is a separate doctrine from that of Transubstantiation.

But the Real Presence is necessarily contained in Transubstantiation.

The Council of Trent

After the revolt of the Protestant reformers in the sixteenth century, the General Council of Trent was assembled by the Catholic Church to define the true teaching of the Church on the Eucharist and on other important matters. It defined the Eucharist as sacrifice as follows: '[Christ] Our Lord and God, was once and for all to offer himself to God the Father by his death on the altar of the cross, to accomplish there an everlasting redemption. But because his priesthood was not to end with his death, at the Last Supper "on the night when he was betrayed", [he wanted] to leave to his beloved spouse the Church a visible sacrifice (as the nature of man demands) by which the bloody sacrifice which he was to accomplish once for all on the cross would be re-presented, its memory perpetuated, until the end of the world, and its salutary power be applied to the forgiveness of the sins we daily commit.' (*CCC*, p. 1366)

The Council also defined the changing of the bread and wine into the Body and Blood of Christ: 'Because Christ our Redeemer said that it was truly his Body that he was offering under the species of bread, it has always been the conviction of the Church of God, and this holy Council now declares again, that by the consecration of bread and wine there takes place a change of the whole substance of the bread into the substance of the Body of Christ our Lord and the whole substance of the wine into the substance of his Blood.

This change the holy Catholic Church has fittingly and properly called transubstantiation.' (*CCC*, p. 1376)

The Word 'Substance'

The word 'substance' belongs to the science of metaphysics, or, first philosophy. It was used by philosophers of ancient Greece and later by Catholic philosophers and theologians, especially in the Middle Ages. It was used by the bishops at the Council of Trent, and is still used in modern times. It has maintained the same precise meaning through the centuries. It means the fundamental basis of being, or the inner essence of being, which is not perceptible to the senses. The 'accidentals', such as shape, colour, visibility, are not realities in themselves; they are only manifestations of the hidden substance of being.

'Modern Science'

To the objection raised by some people that as substance is not perceptible to the senses, therefore it has no reality, the answer is simple. Modern science deals only with part of reality. There are other sciences that deal with things that are not perceptible to the senses – things such as goodness, the human soul and spiritual beings. Though not perceptible to the senses, these things are all realities, and are studied by sciences such as metaphysics, first philosophy and theology. 'Modern Science' is the science of physics with its related sciences. It studies only material things that are perceptible to the senses with or without scientific instruments. Physicists who have confined themselves to the study of material things are outside their ambit of competence in making judgements on things that pertain to philosophy and theology.

In 1961 when the first manned satellite was put into orbit round the earth, the absurdity of the argument from modern science against the real Presence of Christ in the Eucharist was manifested; a similar argument from modern science was used allegedly to prove that there is no God. In regard to the satellite, the argument was put forward that, as the scientific instruments used aboard the satellite found no trace of God in outer space, therefore there was no God. This was an obvious absurdity.

In regard to the Eucharist, the substance of the consecrated Host is the Body of the risen Christ, and is not perceptible to the senses or to any scientific instrument. The risen Body of Christ was not visible to people except to the people that Jesus himself had chosen to see him.

It is worthy of note that many physicist scientists who are versed in philosophy or theology have no difficulty in accepting the word 'substance', as applied to the Eucharist.

Dissension

Dissenting from the teaching of Jesus Christ on the Eucharist in modern times is nothing new. The reason given for unbelief in the Eucharist by the Jews who heard Jesus speaking was, 'How can this man give us his flesh to eat?' (Jn 6:52). The reason given by many of Jesus' own disciples was, 'This is a hard saying: who can listen to it?' The Protestant reformers of the sixteenth century rejected the doctrine of 'Transubstantiation', thereby rejecting the teaching that Jesus changes bread and wine into his Body and Blood. Those who reject Transubstantiation in modern times have composed new words, 'Transignification' and 'Transfinalisation' to replace the word 'Transubstantiation'. Both these words reject the teaching that Jesus changes bread and wine into his Body and Blood. The basis for unbelief in Transubstantiation by all the groups from the time of Jesus to the present is a lack of faith in the truth of the word of Jesus and in his power to do what he promised. The apostle Peter and first Pope was the first follower of Christ to profess his faith in the Eucharist: 'Lord, to whom shall we go? You have the words of eternal life; and we have believed, and have come to know that you are the Holy One of God.' (Jn 6:67-69) His example has been followed by his successors and the successors of the apostles and by all faithful members of the Catholic Church.

The Second Vatican Council

The Second Vatican Council teaches the same doctrine as that of the Council of Trent on the Eucharist, both as sacrifice and as sacrament. Only the way of presenting the doctrine is different. The following is from Vatican II: 'At the Last Supper, on the night when he was betrayed, our Saviour instituted the Eucharistic Sacrifice of his Body and Blood. He did this in order to perpetuate the sacrifice of the cross throughout the centuries until he should come again, and so to entrust to his beloved spouse, the Church, a memorial of his death and Resurrection: a sacrament of love, a sign of unity, a bond of charity, a paschal banquet in which Christ is consumed, the mind is filled with grace, and a pledge of future glory is given to us.' (Liturgy, 47)

Under the Appearances of Bread and Wine
New Mode of Being – A Sacramental Mode

In the unchanged appearance of bread and wine Jesus assumes a new mode of being, a sacramental mode, which enables him to give his flesh to eat and his blood to drink, in the literal sense, without the possibility of a cannibalistic interpretation. This new, sacramental mode of being was, from the beginning, part of God's plan of salvation. It was prefigured in the sacrifice of bread and wine offered by Melchizesedek.

Extract from the Letter of Pope John Paul II on The Mystery and Worship of the Holy Eucharist, 1980:

> Since therefore the Eucharist is the source of charity, it has always been at the centre of the life of Christ's disciples. It has the appearance of bread and wine, that is to say, of food and drink; it is therefore as familiar to the people, as closely linked to their life as food and drink. The veneration of God, who is Love, springs, in Eucharistic worship, from that kind of intimacy in which he himself, by analogy with food and drink, fills our spiritual being, ensuring its life, as food and

drink do. This 'Eucharistic' veneration of God therefore strictly corresponds to his saving plan. (para. 7)

The Foretaste of Heaven

Jesus said, 'He who eats my flesh and drinks my blood abides in me, and I in him' (Jn 6:56). In Holy Communion Jesus gives himself in an intimate union of love with his Church and with each individual faithful communicant. This is the foretaste of heaven. The heavenly liturgy perfects the earthly liturgy. In the Marriage of the Lamb in heaven Jesus gives himself eternally in the perfect, intimate union of love with his redeemed Church and with each redeemed member of that Church. 'Blessed are those who are invited to the Marriage Supper of the Lamb.' (Rev 19:9)

The Mass – Sacrifice and Sacred Sacrificial Meal

'The Mass is at the same time, and inseparably, the sacrificial memorial in which the sacrifice of the Cross is perpetuated, and the sacred banquet of communion with the Lord's body and blood.' (*CCC*, p. 1382)

'The Eucharistic Banquet is truly a "sacred" banquet, in which the simplicity of the signs conceals the unfathomless holiness of God: "O sacred banquet in which Christ is consumed!".' (Pope John Paul II, *Ecclesia de Eucharistia*, 48)

The Priestly Prayer of Jesus

After Jesus had instituted the Eucharist at the Last Supper in which he anticipated his sacrifice on the cross, before he entered Gethsemane to begin the agony of his Passion, he prayed to his heavenly Father, as the Eternal Priest of the Eternal Sacrifice, the prayer called the Priestly Prayer of Jesus. 'He lifted up his eyes to heaven and said, "Father, the hour has come, glorify thy Son, that the Son may glorify thee, since thou hast given him power over all flesh, to give eternal life to all whom thou hast given him. And this is eternal life, that they know thee the only true God and Jesus Christ whom thou hast sent. I glorified thee on earth, having accomplished the work which thou gavest me to do; and now, Father, glorify thou me in thy own presence with the glory which I had before the world was made".' (Jn 17:1-5)

The ministry of Jesus on earth and his Passion and Death, offered in loving obedience to his Father and out of love for the whole world, glorified his Father in heaven; his heavenly Father glorified Jesus his divine Son with the glorious Resurrection and Ascension to the glory which he had before the world was made.

The Triumph of Good over Evil
His Holiness Pope Benedict XVI in his homily during Mass on World Youth Day in Cologne on 21 August 2005 explains the central meaning of the Eucharist. The following is an extract from the homily:

> How can Jesus distribute his Body and Blood? By making the bread into his Body and the wine into his Blood, he anticipates his death, he accepts it in his heart and he transforms it into an action of love. What on the outside is simply brutal violence, from within becomes an action of total self-giving love. This is the substantial transformation which was accomplished at the Last Supper and was destined to set in motion a series of transformations leading ultimately to the transformation of the world, when God will be all in all (cf. 1 Cor 15:28). In their hearts, people always and everywhere have somehow expected a change, a transformation of the world. Here now is the central act of transformation that alone can truly renew the world: violence is transformed into love, and death into life. Since this act transmutes death into love, death as such is already conquered from within, the resurrection is already present in it. Death is, so to speak, mortally wounded, so that it can no longer have the last word. To use an image well known to us today, this is like inducing nuclear fission in the very heart of being – the victory of love over hatred, the victory of love

over death. Only this intimate explosion of good conquering evil can then trigger off the series of transformations that little by little will change the world. All other changes remain superficial and cannot save. For this reason we speak of redemption: what had to happen at the most intimate level has indeed happened, and as we can enter into its dynamic, Jesus can distribute his Body, because he truly gives himself.[1]

Note on the Passover Meal

Throughout the Passover meal, at four different stages, those present drank a cup of wine mixed with water, at each stage. St Luke refers, in his account, to the second cup, the cup which Jesus consecrated. This second cup was the only cup of wine consecrated by Jesus.

In St Luke's account, Jesus says, 'I tell you that from now on I shall not drink of the fruit of the vine until the Kingdom of God comes'. This means that this is the last time that Jesus will celebrate the Passover. It is being superseded by the Eucharist, which Jesus is now about to institute.

The Eucharist – The Fulfilment of Prefigurations, Prophecies, Symbols

The institution of the Blessed Eucharist is the fulfilment, the actualisation, of the prefigurations, prophecies and symbols revealed by God in the Old Testament. God revealed his plan of salvation gradually down through the generations from the first Adam to the coming of the Second Adam, the Messias, Jesus Christ. Jesus Christ was himself the final revelation and the fulfilment of all the prophecies and other forms of revelation in the Old Testament. Jesus knew he was the Messias; he knew his Father's plan of salvation; he knew all that was written in the scriptures about this plan; he knew the role that his Father had given to him in this plan; he willingly accepted this role out of love for his Father, even during his Passion; in his prayer to his heavenly Father in Gethsemane he said, 'Not my will but thine be done'. He offered himself on the cross in the sacrifice of love for his Father and his love for the people of the world. He fulfilled the promise he made in Capernaum, when he instituted the Eucharist and gave his flesh to eat and his blood to drink under the appearance of bread and wine.

* * *

THE PASSION AND DEATH OF JESUS CHRIST

The Commitment at His Baptism

On entering the water of the Jordan to be baptised by John, Jesus, in loving obedience to his Father's will, took upon himself the sins of the world, to atone for them, and to redeem the world. After the baptism the heavens were opened and the Spirit of God descended on Jesus and alighted on him. The voice of God the Father in heaven was heard saying, 'This is my beloved, with whom I am well pleased' (Mt 3:16-17). With the baptism of Jesus the divine plan of salvation was publicly inaugurated by the Blessed Trinity. Next day John the Baptist introduced Jesus to the people, proclaiming, 'Behold, the Lamb of God who takes away the sin of the world' (Jn 1:29).

The Passion

The word 'passion' comes from the Latin word *passio*, which means 'suffering'. As applied to Jesus it means his suffering from the Last Supper on Thursday night through Friday morning to his crucifixion and death on Friday afternoon.

Why did Jesus have to suffer?

The preaching by Jesus of the truth of the Good News led to the opposition of the Jewish authorities and to his suffering and death. God permitted this to happen, in order to bring about the glorification of Jesus Christ in his resurrection, and in order to make reparation to God the Father for the sins of the world, and to enable all people to enjoy eventually the happiness of heaven. The mystery of Jesus' passion, death and resurrection is the central part of the mystery of God's plan of salvation. For the sake of the salvation of the whole world, God permitted the passion and death of his Son that resulted from the blindness of his enemies. In his first sermon in Jerusalem after the resurrection, Peter declared, 'This Jesus was delivered up according to the definite plan and foreknowledge of God' (Acts 2:23).

The scriptures had foretold God's plan of salvation. Jesus suffered and died that 'the scriptures might be fulfilled'. St Paul states that 'Christ died for our sins in accordance with the scriptures' (1 Cor 15:3). The sufferings and death of Jesus were caused by the sins of the whole world. It is not true to say that the Jews alone were responsible for the Lord's passion and death. The Second Vatican Council declares: 'Neither all Jews indiscriminately at that time, nor Jews today can be charged with the crimes committed during his Passion … The Jews should not be spoken of as rejected or accursed as if this followed from Holy Scripture.' (*CCC*, p. 597)

The Gospel Accounts of the Passion of Our Lord Jesus Christ

In the Liturgy of the Mass on Passion Sunday one of the three synoptic accounts of the Passion of Our Lord Jesus Christ is read: Matthew's account is read in Cycle A, Mark's is read in Cycle B, Luke's is read in Cycle C. On Good Friday John's account is read every year. All four accounts could be summarised under the five Sorrowful Mysteries of the Rosary: the Agony in the Garden, the Scourging at the Pillar, the Crowning with Thorns, the Carrying of the Cross to Calvary, the Crucifixion and Death of the Lord.

The Agony in the Garden

After the Last Supper, Jesus and the apostles went to the Garden of Gethsemane; he said to them, 'Sit here, while I go yonder and pray'. And taking with him Peter and James and John, he began to be sorrowful and troubled. He said to them, 'My soul is very sorrowful, even to death'. Then he knelt and prayed, 'My Father, if it be possible, let this cup pass from me; nevertheless, not as I will, but as thou wilt' … 'And there appeared to him an angel from heaven strengthening him. And being in an agony, he prayed more earnestly; and his sweat became like great drops of blood falling down upon the ground.'

Fear of the sufferings he was about to endure affected the human will of Jesus, but fear did not change his determination to do his Father's will. After Jesus had resisted the temptations of the devil in the desert, the devil 'departed from him until an opportune time'. The opportune time had come when Jesus was entering into his passion. After the temptations in the desert, 'angels came and ministered to him'. After Jesus had prayed in Gethsemane to his Father, 'there appeared to him an angel from heaven strengthening him'.

'His sweat became like great drops of blood falling down upon the ground.' The sweating of blood was caused by the intense agony of Jesus which caused his blood to flow out through the pores of his flesh. This was the first outpouring of the blood of Jesus in his passion.

Jesus came to the apostles and found them sleeping; he said to Peter, 'So, could you not watch with me one hour? Watch and pray that you may not enter into temptation; the spirit indeed is willing, but the flesh is weak'. He went away and prayed for the second time, 'My Father, if this cannot pass unless I drink it, thy will be done'. And again, for the second time he came and found them sleeping, 'for their eyes were heavy'. He went away for the third time and prayed as before. Then for the third time he came to the disciples and said to them, 'Are you still sleeping and taking your rest? Behold, the hour is at hand, and the Son of Man is betrayed into the hands of sinners. Rise, let us be going; see, my betrayer is at hand'.

Jesus is arrested in the Garden of Gethsemane
While Jesus was still speaking, Judas, one of the apostles, came, and with him a great crowd with swords and clubs, from the chief priests and the elders of the people. Judas had given them a sign,

saying, 'The one I shall kiss is the man; seize him'. Judas came up to Jesus, and said, 'Hail, Master!' And he kissed him. Jesus said to him, 'Judas, would you betray the Son of Man with a kiss?' Then Peter, who had a sword, drew it and struck the slave of the high priest and cut off his ear. Jesus said to him, 'Put your sword back into its place; for all who take the sword will perish by the sword. Do you think that I cannot appeal to my Father, and he will at once send me more than twelve legions of angels? But how then should the scriptures be fulfilled, that it must be so?' At that hour Jesus said to the crowds, 'Have you come out as against a robber, with swords and clubs to capture me? Day after day I sat in the temple teaching, and you did not seize me. But all this has taken place, that the scriptures of the prophets might be fulfilled'. Then all the disciples forsook him and fled.

Jesus is brought before the Jewish Council

Jesus was led first to Annas, the preceding high priest, and then to Caiaphas, the reigning high priest. The high priests and the whole Jewish Council sought false testimony against Jesus that they might put him to death. Jesus remained silent. Then the high priest said to him, 'I adjure you by the living God, tell us if you are the Christ, the Son of God'. Jesus replied, 'You have said so. But I tell you, hereafter you will see the Son of Man seated at the right hand of Power, and coming in the clouds of heaven'. Then the high priest tore his robes, and said, 'He has uttered blasphemy. Why do we still need witnesses? You have now heard his blasphemy. What is your judgement?' They answered, 'He deserves death'. Then they spat in his face, and struck him; and some slapped him, saying, 'Prophesy to us, you Christ! Who is it that struck you?'

The Jewish Council broke the law by holding a trial during the hours of darkness.

Peter's Denials

On three different occasions before different people in the precincts of the high priest's residence, Peter denied that he knew Jesus.

Immediately after the third denial the cock crowed. And the Lord turned and looked at Peter. And Peter remembered the saying of Jesus, 'Before the cock crows, you will deny me three times', and Peter went out and wept bitterly.

Jesus is brought before Pilate
At daybreak the chief priests with the elders and scribes and the whole council held another meeting to decide on the best way to get Pilate, the Roman Governor, to ratify the death sentence on Jesus. According to the Law of Rome the Jewish authorities did not have the authority to carry out the death sentence. It was necessary to have the sentence ratified by the Governor.

The Trial before Pilate
Pilate conducted his own interrogation before deciding on the case. To the Jewish authorities he said:

'What accusation do you bring against this man?'

The Jews: 'If this man were not an evil-doer we would not have handed him over.'

Pilate: 'Take him yourselves and judge him by your own law.'

The Jews: 'It is not lawful for us to put any man to death.'

Pilate to Jesus: 'Are you the King of the Jews?'

Jesus: 'Do you say this of your own accord, or did others say it to you about me?'

Pilate: 'Am I a Jew? Your own nation and the chief priests have handed you over to me; what have you done?'

Jesus: 'My kingdom is not of this world; if my kingship were of this world, my servants would fight, that I might not be handed over to the Jews; but my kingship is not of this world.'

Pilate: 'So you are a king?'

Jesus: 'You say that I am a king. For this I was born, and for this I have come into the world, to bear witness to the truth. Every one who is of the truth hears my voice.'

Pilate: 'What is truth?'

After this Pilate went out to the Jews and told them, 'I find no cause in him'. He was willing to release Jesus. But the Jews replied: 'He stirs up the people, teaching throughout all Judea, from Galilee to this place.'

When Pilate heard that Jesus was from Galilee, which was in Herod's jurisdiction, he sent Jesus to Herod, who was in Jerusalem at that time.

Jesus before Herod

Herod questioned Jesus at some length, but Jesus made no answer. 'Then Herod with his soldiers treated him with contempt and mocked him; then arraying him in gorgeous apparel, he sent him back to Pilate.'

Pilate tries again to release Jesus

Pilate then called together the chief priests and rulers and the people. He said, 'I did not find this man guilty of any of your charges against him; neither did Herod, for he sent him back to us. Behold, nothing deserving death has been done by him. I will therefore chastise him and release him'.

After this, Pilate said to the Jews, 'You have a custom that I should release one man for you at the Passover; will you have me release for you the King of the Jews?' They cried out, 'Not this man but Barrabas!' Barrabas was a robber.

The Scourging of Jesus and the Crowning with Thorns

'Then Pilate took Jesus and scourged him. And the soldiers plaited a crown of thorns, and put it on his head, and arrayed him in a purple robe; they came up to him saying, "Hail, King of the Jews" and struck him with their hands.' In reporting the events of Christ's Passion the evangelists refrain from giving the painful details. In reporting the scourging, which was a frightful punishment, St John simply says, 'Then Pilate took Jesus and scourged him'. No details are given. It would seem that for the evangelists, even the mention of the scourging was so painful that they hurried over the words.

It is known from the secular historians of ancient Rome that there was no limit to the number of strokes that could be inflicted on a victim, and that in some cases the victim died under the strokes. In Jewish law the number of strokes to be given was limited to thirty-nine. It was normal to administer scourging before crucifixion.

The crowning with thorns was not part of the official punishment. It was inflicted on Jesus by soldiers of the garrison to cause further pain to Jesus and to provide amusement for all the soldiers present in the praetorium.

Ecce Homo

After this Pilate brought Jesus out on the balcony before the people. He said, 'Behold, I am bringing him out to you that you may know that I find no crime in him'. So Jesus came out wearing the crown of thorns and the purple robe. Pilate said to the people, in Latin, '*Ecce Homo*', which is translated, 'Here is the man!' or, 'Behold the man!' When the chief priests and the officers saw Jesus, they cried out, 'Crucify him, crucify him'. Pilate sought to release him, but the Jews cried out, 'If you release this man, you are not Caesar's friend; every one who makes himself a king sets himself against Caesar'. When Pilate heard these words, he brought Jesus out and sat down on the judgement seat. He said to the Jews, 'Here is your king!' They cried out, 'Away with him, crucify him!' Pilate said, 'Shall I crucify your king?' The chief priests answered, 'We have no king but Caesar'. Then Pilate handed Jesus over to them to be crucified.

The Way of the Cross, the Sorrowful Way

The Way of the Cross, the Sorrowful Way, was the painful journey travelled by Jesus carrying his cross from Pilate's Hall to Calvary. From earliest times the devotion to follow in the footsteps of Jesus in his sorrowful way to Calvary was practised by Christian pilgrims. A desire to reproduce the Holy Place in other lands started for those who could not visit the Holy Land, as early as the fifth century, and it gradually became a complete devotion in itself. In the development of the devotion in other lands there was much variety in the number of stations and the particular scenes manifested. In 1584 a book written by Adrichomius gives twelve stations as the number for the devotion; these twelve stations correspond exactly with the first twelve stations of the present time. In 1731 Pope Clement XII fixed the number of stations at fourteen. The following are the fourteen stations:

1. Jesus is condemned to death
2. Jesus receives the cross
3. Jesus falls the first time under the weight of the cross
4. Jesus meets his Blessed Mother
5. Simon of Cyrene is compelled to carry the cross behind Jesus
6. Veronica wipes the face of Jesus with a towel
7. Jesus falls the second time
8. The women of Jerusalem mourn for Jesus
9. Jesus falls the third time
10. Jesus is stripped of his garments
11. Jesus is nailed to the cross
12. Jesus dies on the cross
13. The body of Jesus is taken down from the cross and laid in the arms of his Blessed Mother
14. The body of Jesus is laid in the tomb.[2]

The Stations of the Cross

The exercise of the Stations of the Cross is one of the most popular devotions of the Catholic Church. It enables people more effectively to obey Jesus Christ's injunction to take up our cross and follow him. Of the fourteen scenes displayed in the Station pictures nine are scenes recorded in the Gospels; the other five – Jesus meets his Mother, Jesus falls three times, Veronica wipes the face of Jesus – are not explicitly recorded in the Gospels; they are based on ancient traditions which are implicit in the Gospel accounts. The Gospels did not explicitly record every detail.

The Women of Jerusalem and the Women of Galilee

Amongst the hostile crowd that followed Jesus to Calvary were two groups of women who mourned him. First the women of Jerusalem: 'And there followed him a great multitude of the people, and of women who bewailed and lamented him. But Jesus turning to them said, "Daughters of Jerusalem, do not weep for me, but weep for yourselves and for your children".' (Lk 23:27-28)

'There were also women looking on from afar, among whom were Mary Magdalene, and Mary the mother of James the younger and of Joses, and Salome, and also many other women who came up with him to Jerusalem.' (Mk 15:40-41)

Jesus is met by his Mother

From St Luke we learn that the women of Jerusalem were able to get so near to Jesus that they could talk to him, and he was able to reply. From St Mark we learn that the women from Galilee 'looked on from afar'. Mark names two of the women from Galilee, but he does not mention Mary the Mother of Jesus; the question is, where was Mary the Mother of Jesus? The answer can only be that Mary the Mother of Jesus was among the multitude that followed Jesus to Calvary. The man carrying his cross to Calvary was her son, Jesus, and nothing would stop her from going through the people, and getting near to her son, near enough to speak to him. The tradition says that Mary met her son Jesus carrying his cross to Calvary. The event is recorded in the Fourth Station of the Way of the Cross.

In the fourth Gospel St John records that after the crucifixion, 'standing by the cross of Jesus were his Mother, and his Mother's sister, Mary the wife of Clopas, and Mary Magdalene' (Jn 19:25). The two women of Galilee named by Mark joined the Mother of Jesus at the foot of the cross. The meeting of Mary with her Son on the road to Calvary is implicit in the Gospel account of the Passion of Christ.

Jesus falls under the Cross

Considering the events of the long night after the Last Supper and the long morning the next day – the Agony of Jesus in Gethsemane, his arrest and the trial in the house of Caiaphas, the physical ill-treatment before and after the trial, the trials before Pilate, and Herod, and before Pilate again, the scourging and the crowning with thorns – one can say that the wonder is that Jesus was still alive. His physical condition was such that he was not able to carry the cross. He did not refuse to carry the cross; he welcomed it. He was determined to carry the cross until his physical strength was so exhausted that he fell to the ground. He would have fallen several times before the soldiers decided he was not able to carry the cross, and that he would die on the way, and that there would be no crucifixion, if they continued to force him to get up every time he fell. 'And as they led him away, they seized one Simon of Cyrene, who was coming in from the country, and laid on him the cross, to carry it behind Jesus.' (Lk 23:26)

A strong tradition states that Jesus fell several times on his way to Calvary; there was no unanimity on the number of times. Church authority finally decided that the number was three. The three falls are commemorated in the Third, Seventh and Ninth Stations. Apart from the tradition, the falls can be deduced from the Gospel accounts of the Passion of Jesus.

Veronica – The Image of Christ on the Towel

Veronica was the name given to one of the women of Jerusalem who bewailed and lamented Jesus on his sorrowful way to Calvary. She is not mentioned in the Gospels, but there is a strong and widespread tradition that one of the holy women of Jerusalem had such compassion for Jesus that she approached him as he was carrying the cross, and wiped his face with a towel. Jesus rewarded here compassion by leaving the impression of his sacred face on the towel. According to the tradition, this woman later went to Rome, bringing the image with her. It was received by the early Christians with great veneration. With the passing of time, devotion to the image spread through all Italy and France and other regions in Europe. So many copies of the image were made that it became necessary to declare that the image in Rome was the only true image. The Latin words for 'true image' are *vera icon*. In time the common usage of these two words combined them into one word – Veronica. The word 'Veronica' meant the true image of Christ.

Much later the word was mistakenly thought to be the name of the woman who received the true image from Christ. Before her death Veronica bequeathed the sacred image to Pope Clement and his successors. It is not known what happened to the image. It may have been lost in the persecutions of the early Christians in Rome.

The Devotion given to the Image

The image inspired remarkable devotion to the Passion of Jesus Christ. It was considered to be a portrait of the suffering Christ which was sketched by Christ himself with his own blood. Even though St Veronica and the sacred image are not recorded in the Gospels, the tradition concerning them is so strong, and the resulting devotion has been so spiritually beneficial, that the tradition is worthy of credence.[3]

The Final Stage of the Sorrowful Way

After the third fall at the ninth station, Jesus was led by the soldiers on to the summit of Mount Calvary. The events which took place on Calvary are recorded in the Gospel narrative and are depicted in the Stations of the Cross, from the tenth to the fourteenth, inclusive.

The Crucifixion and Death of the Lord

The soldiers offered Jesus wine to drink, mingled with gall; but when he tasted it, he would not drink it. They stripped him of his garments. Then they crucified him. They also crucified two criminals, one on the right side and one on the left of Jesus. Pilate wrote the title which was put on the cross, 'Jesus of Nazareth the King of the Jews'. The chief priests said to Pilate, 'Do not write, "The King of the Jews", but, 'this man said, "I am the King of the

Jews"'. Pilate answered, 'What I have written I have written'. When the soldiers had crucified Jesus, they took his garments and made four parts, one for each soldier; his tunic was without seam, woven from top to bottom; so they said to one another, 'Let us not tear it, but cast lots for it to see whose it shall be'. This was to fulfil the scripture in psalm 22: 'They parted my garments among them and for my clothing they cast lots.' When Jesus was led to Calvary for his crucifixion and death, the prophecy of Isaias was fulfilled: 'Like a lamb that is led to the slaughter, and like a sheep that before its shearers is dumb, so he opened not his mouth.' (Isa 53:7)

The Mockery of Jesus on the Cross

Those who passed by derided Jesus on the cross, wagging their heads and saying: 'You who would destroy the temple and build it in three days, save yourself! If you are the Son of God, come down from the cross.' The chief priests with the scribes and elders also mocked him, saying, 'He saved others; he cannot save himself. He is the King of Israel; let him come down now from the cross, and we will believe in him. He trusts in God, let God deliver him now, if he desires him; for he said, "I am the Son of God"'. The criminals who were crucified with him also reviled him. This mockery was foretold in psalm 22:

> But I am a worm and no man; scorned by men, and despised
> by the people.
> All who see me mock at me,
> they make mouths at me, they wag their heads.
> He committed his cause to the Lord; let him deliver him,
> let him rescue him, for he delights in him.

The Seven Words of Jesus on the Cross

The enemies of Jesus brought about the crucifixion and death of an innocent man; for this they were guilty and were in need of forgiveness. Jesus knew that they did not believe they were crucifying the Son of God. Their ignorance was a mitigating circumstance. From the cross Jesus prayed, 'Father, forgive them for they know not what they do'.

In praying for the forgiveness of his enemies, Jesus was giving a sublime example of the forgiveness he preached to the people. In the Lord's Prayer which he taught, we pray, 'Forgive us our trespasses as we forgive those who trespass against us'. Jesus said, 'For if you forgive men their trespasses, your heavenly father will also forgive you; but if you do not forgive men their trespasses, neither will your Father forgive your trespasses' (Mt 6:14-15). Jesus also taught, 'Love your enemies and pray for those who persecute you' (Mt 5:44).

'Today you will be with me in Paradise'

One of the two criminals angrily complained to Jesus, 'Are you not the Christ? Save yourself and us'. But the other rebuked him saying, 'Do you not fear God since you are under the same sentence of condemnation? And we indeed justly, for we are receiving the due rewards of our deeds; but this man has done nothing wrong'. And he said, 'Jesus, remember me, when you come into your kingly power'. Jesus said to him, 'Truly, I say to you, today you will be with me in Paradise'.

The repentant sinner only asks Jesus to remember him. Jesus gives him the greatest gift that could be given. In this divine gift there was full forgiveness and undescribable reward.

'Woman, behold, your son!' – 'Behold, your mother'

'Standing by the cross of Jesus were his Mother, and his Mother's Sister, Mary the wife of Clopas, and Mary Magdalene. When Jesus saw his Mother and the disciple whom he loved standing near, he said to his Mother, "Woman, behold, your son!" Then he said to the disciple, "Behold, your Mother!" And from that hour the disciple took her to his own home.' (Jn 19:25-27)

From the cross Jesus addressed his Mother as Woman. He had already given her that title at the wedding feast of Cana. On the cross the title had a deeper meaning. In the Book of Genesis God rebuked the serpent (Satan) saying, 'I will put enmity between you and the woman, and between your seed and her seed; he will bruise your head and you shall bruise his heel' (Gen 3:15). In this divine Promise the woman whose seed will bruise the head of the serpent is Mary the Mother of Jesus the Redeemer. Jesus will destroy the power of the serpent by bruising its head. The serpent will be allowed to cause temporary suffering to Jesus by bruising his heel.

The divine Promise in the Book of Genesis also states, 'I will put enmity between you and the woman'. From the beginning, God had planned that Mary would have a special, subordinate, role with her Son in the work of the Redemption. She was exercising that special role when she stood at the foot of the cross, suffering with her Son, lovingly consenting to the sacrifice her Son was offering of himself on the cross for the redemption of the world.

Behold, your Son – Behold, your Mother
As Mary was the Mother of the Redeemer, she became the spiritual Mother of all the redeemed. As John became the spiritual son of Mary, he represented all Mary's spiritual children at the foot of the cross.

John the Adopted Member of the Holy Family
After the death of Jesus, Mary was the only remaining member of the Holy Family. From the cross Jesus made the beloved disciple John an adopted member of that family. His first responsibility was to be the Protector of his spiritual Mother. 'And from that hour the disciple took her to his own home.' (Jn 19:27)

'My God, My God, why hast thou forsaken me?'
'And when the sixth hour had come, there was darkness over the whole land until the ninth hour. And at the ninth hour Jesus cried out with a loud voice, "*Eloi, Eloi, lama sabachthani?*", which means, "My God, my God, why hast thou forsaken me?"' (Lk 15:33-24)

These words spoken by Jesus from the cross are the first verse of psalm 22. They are an expression of faith and trust in God by a faithful disciple of God for help in extreme pain. Jesus made these words his own, when he was suffering the most extreme pain in body and soul on the cross; as the words were the first verse of the psalm, he was intoning the meaning of the whole psalm. The first part describes his sufferings, the second part is an expression of his trust in God his heavenly father. During his agony in Gethsemane Jesus prayed to his Father. 'And there appeared to him an angel from heaven, strengthening him.' (Lk 22:43) On the cross Jesus also prayed to his Father, and his prayer was heard.

'*I thirst*'

After this, Jesus, knowing that all was now about to be accomplished, said, to fulfil the scripture, 'I thirst'. The verse in scripture that is being fulfilled is in psalm 69:21: 'They gave me poison for food, and for my thirst they gave me vinegar to drink.'

The thirst that Jesus was experiencing was due to his loss of blood and dehydration. But there is a deeper meaning to his thirst. Jesus knows that he is about to die. He has successfully overcome the agonies of his passion and the temptations of the evil spirit in his darkest hour. His great thirst is for re-union with his Father in heaven. His thirst for God is described in scripture:

> As a hart longs for flowing streams,
> so longs my soul for thee, O God.
> My soul thirsts for God, for the living God.
> When shall I come and behold the face of God? (Ps 42)

The thirst of Jesus also expresses his desire to save his people for whom he lays down his life on the cross.

'*It is Finished*'

A bowl full of vinegar stood there; so they put a sponge full of vinegar on a hyssop and held it to his mouth. When the vinegar was given to him, Jesus said, 'It is finished'. Jesus is saying that out of love for his Father he has finished the work that his Father gave him to do; he has fulfilled all that was written about him in the scriptures. As the Father loved the world, so did he, his divine Son, love the world. 'He had always loved those who were his, and now he showed the full extent of his love.'

'Father, into thy Hands I commit my Spirit'
It was now about the sixth hour, and there was darkness over the whole land until the ninth hour, while the sun's light failed; and the curtain of the temple was torn in two. Then Jesus, crying with a loud voice, said, 'Father, into thy hands I commit my spirit!' And having said this, he breathed his last.

After the Death of Jesus
When Jesus breathed his last, the curtain of the temple was torn in two, the earth shook, the rocks were split, the tombs were opened and many bodies of the saints who had died were raised. The centurion who was on guard with soldiers said, 'Truly, this man was the Son of God'. The multitude who had assembled to see the sight returned home beating their breasts.

One of the soldiers pierced his side with a spear
St John, the beloved disciple, who was at the foot of the cross when Jesus died, records in his Gospel: 'One of the soldiers pierced his side with a spear, and at once there came out blood and water … For these things took place that the scriptures might be fulfilled, "Not a bone of him shall be broken".' And again another scripture says, 'They shall look on him whom they have pierced' (Jn 19:34, 36, 37).

The curtain of the temple was torn in two. This symbolised the end of the Old and the beginning of the New Covenant. The New Covenant was ratified by the blood of Christ. The inauguration of the Church is symbolised by the blood and water which flowed from the open side of the crucified Christ (cf. Vatican II, *The Church*, 3).

The Role of Mary, Mother of Jesus

When the soldier pierced the side of Jesus with a spear, he also pierced the soul of Mary. The prophecy of Simeon was fulfilled: 'and a sword will pierce through your own soul also.' (Lk 2:35) By her participation in the sacrifice of her Son, Mary became the New Eve, the Mother of all the living, the Mother of the Church, the Woman of the Eucharist (cf. *CCC*, pp. 2617–8).

Thirteenth Station – The Body of Jesus is taken down from the Cross
Fourteenth Station – The Body of Jesus is laid in the Tomb

When Pilate had been informed that Jesus was already dead, he gave permission that the body be taken down. Joseph of Arimathea, a disciple of Jesus, and Nichodemus, who had at first come to Jesus by night, took down the body of Jesus from the cross and laid it in the arms of his Mother. Joseph and Nichodemus wrapped the body in a clean linen shroud, and along with other cloths and spices, they laid it in Joseph's own tomb which he had hewn in a rock in a garden near the place where Jesus was crucified. Then they rolled a great stone to the door of the tomb and departed. Mary Magdalene and Mary the Mother of James the younger and of Joses saw where he was laid.

The Tomb is guarded and sealed

The day after the burial of Jesus the high priests and the Pharisees went to Pilate and said, 'Sir, we remember how that impostor said, while he was still alive, "After three days I will rise again". Therefore order the sepulchre to be made secure until the third day, lest his disciples go and steal him away, and tell the people, "He has risen from the dead", and the last fraud will be worse than the first'. Pilate gave them permission to put a guard of soldiers on the tomb and to make it secure. So they put a guard on the tomb and they sealed the stone.

The Sorrows of Mary, the Mother of the Redeemer

1. The Prophecy of Simeon: 'Behold, this child is set for the fall

and rising of many in Israel, and for a sign that is spoken against, and a sword will pierce through your own soul also.'

2. The Flight into Egypt: 'An angel of the Lord appeared to Joseph in a dream and said, "Rise and take the child and his Mother, and flee to Egypt, and remain there till I tell you; for Herod is about to search for the child, to destroy him".'

3. Searching for the twelve-year-old boy, Jesus, when he was lost for three days in Jerusalem.

4. Meeting Jesus on the way to Calvary, when he was carrying the cross on which he was to die.

5. Standing at the foot of the cross while Jesus was suffering the pains of crucifixion.

6. Embracing in her arms the dead body of her Son taken down from the cross.

7. Seeing the burial of her Son in the tomb.

The Horror of the Passion of Jesus Christ

The crucifixion of Jesus Christ, God's own Son, his only Son, was the greatest evil committed by human beings in the history of mankind. The crucifixion itself was the most cruel form of execution used by any nation. The crucifixion of Jesus was preceded by scourging, crowning with thorns, mockery and hatred. Some people found it difficult to believe that God would allow his only Son to suffer such outrages; for such people the death of Christ became the 'scandal of the cross'.

The Enormity of Human Sins – The Infinite Love of God

The evil of original sin and the succeeding sins of the world are all offences against God, who is infinitely good in himself; he created human beings to share with them his own love and happiness; the sins of the world against the infinitely holy and infinitely loving God are so horrifying that no human being nor all human beings together could ever make proper reparation or atonement for such evil. Only Jesus Christ, who is God and man, could make the atonement divine justice would require. Jesus Christ, God and

Man, the Saviour of the world, made super-abundant atonement through his sufferings and death on the cross. This atonement by the suffering Redeemer was foretold in the scriptures.

The Passion of Christ proclaims the Mystery of Divine Love
The Passion of Jesus Christ culminating in his death on the cross proclaims the mystery of divine love within the Blessed Trinity, the infinite love of the Father for the Son and the infinite love of the Son for the Father; it also proclaims the mystery of God's love for the people he created in his own image and likeness: 'God so loved the world that he gave his only Son that whoever believes in him should not perish but have eternal life.' (Jn 3:16) Jesus Christ loves the world with a love that is divine and human; he suffered his Passion and Death on the cross out of love for his heavenly Father, and out of love for the peoples of all times. Jesus said, 'Greater love has no man than this that a man lay down his life for his friends' (Jn 15:13). Jesus gave his life for his friends and for his enemies. For his enemies who crucified him he said, 'Father, forgive them, for they know not what they do' … 'For this reason the Father loves me, because I lay down my life, that I may take it again. No one takes it from me, but I lay it down of my own accord. I have power to lay it down, and I have power to take it again. This charge I have received from my Father' (Jn 10:14ff).

* * *

THE RESURRECTION

The Easter Proclamation – Based on the Song of the Israelites and on Psalm 118 and on The New Testament
The Easter Vigil Liturgy is the combined celebration of the mighty victories in both the Old and the New Testaments. The Song of the Israelites was sung after the victorious crossing of the Red Sea (Ex 15:1ff). Psalm 118 was sung in the Temple of Jerusalem for the celebration of the annual feast of the Passover Lamb. The Easter

Vigil Proclamation is based partly on the Song of the Israelites and on Psalm 118. The antiphon, 'This is the day which the Lord has made, let us rejoice and be glad in it', taken from Psalm 118, gives the theme for the Easter Vigil and Easter Day ceremonies. The Easter Proclamation is based principally on the New Testament. It rejoices in the victory of Jesus Christ, the true Lamb of God, over sin and death in his Passion, Death and Resurrection, and in his redeeming of the world.

The following are extracts from the Proclamation:

> Rejoice, heavenly powers! Sing, Choirs of angels!
> Exult, all creation around God's throne!
> Jesus Christ, our King, is risen,
> Sound the trumpet of salvation!

> Rejoice, O earth, in shining splendour,
> radiant in the brightness of your King!
> Christ has conquered! Glory fills you!
> Darkness vanishes for ever!

> Rejoice, O Mother Church! Exult in glory!
> The risen Saviour shines upon you!
> Let this place resound with joy,
> echoing the mighty song of all God's people!

> For Christ has ransomed us with his blood,
> and paid for us the price of Adam's sin
> to our eternal Father!
> This is our passover feast,
> when Christ the true Lamb is slain,
> whose blood consecrates the homes of all believers.

> This is the night when Christians everywhere
> washed clean of sin
> and freed from all defilement

are restored to grace and grow together in holiness.
This is the night when Jesus Christ
broke the chains of death
and rose triumphant from the grave.
(Sunday Missal)

The Gospel Accounts of the Resurrection

All four Gospels narrate the fact of the Resurrection; the following is a summary:

On the first day of the week, when the sun had risen, the day after the Sabbath, and the third day after the burial of Jesus, three holy women, Mary Magdalene, and Mary the mother of James, and Salome, went to the tomb to anoint the body of Jesus. They were wondering who would roll back the large stone from the door of the tomb. But 'there was a great earthquake; for an angel of the Lord descended from heaven, and rolled back the stone, and sat upon it. His appearance was like lightning, and his rainment white as snow. And for fear of him the guards trembled and became like dead men' (Mt 28:2-4). When the women went into the tomb, they did not find the body (Lk 24:3). They were perplexed about this. But then two men in dazzling apparel stood by them. They were frightened and bowed their heads to the ground. The men said to them, 'Why do you seek the living among the dead? Remember how he told you while he was still alive in Galilee that the Son of Man must be delivered into the hands of sinful men, and be crucified, and on the third day rise' (Lk 24:4-7) 'But go, tell his disciples and Peter that he is going before you to Galilee; there you will see him as he told you.' (Mk 16:7) The women told everything to the apostles, but 'these words seemed to them an idle tale and they did not believe them' (Lk 24:11).

Mary Magdalene went to Peter and to John the beloved disciple and said to them, 'They have taken the Lord out of the tomb and we do not know where they have laid him'.

Peter and John both ran to the tomb; John arrived there first, and looking into the tomb, 'he saw the linen cloths lying there, but he did not go in. Then Peter came and went in to the tomb; he saw the linen cloths lying, and the napkin, which had been on his head, not lying with the linen cloths, but rolled up in a place by itself'. John also went in, and he 'saw and believed'. Peter and John then went back to their homes.

'But Mary stood there weeping outside the tomb, and as she wept, she stopped to look into the tomb; and she saw two angels in white, sitting where the body of Jesus had lain, one at the head and one at the feet. They said to her, "Woman, why are you weeping?" She said to them, "Because they have taken away my Lord, and I do not know where they have laid him". Saying this, she turned round and saw Jesus standing. But she did not know that it was Jesus. Jesus said to her, "Woman, why are you weeping? Whom do you seek?" Supposing him to be the gardener, she said to him, "Sir, if you have carried him away, tell me where you have laid him, and I will take him away". Jesus said to her, "Mary". She turned and said to him in Hebrew, "*Raboni*" [which means 'Teacher']. Jesus said to her, "Do not hold me, for I have not yet ascended to my Father and your Father, to my God and your God". Mary Magdalene went and said to the disciples, "I have seen the Lord"; and she told them that he had said these things to her.' (Jn 20:2-18)[4]

The Road to Emmaus

On that day, the first Easter Sunday, two disciples of Jesus were walking to a village named Emmaus about seven miles from Jerusalem.

They were talking about all that had happened over the last few days. While they were talking, 'Jesus himself drew near and went with them. But their eyes were kept from recognising him'. Jesus said to them, 'What is this conversation which you are holding with each other as you walk?' The disciples stood still, looking sad. One of them, names Cleopas, replied, 'Are you the only visitor to Jerusalem who does not know the things that have happened there in these days?' Jesus asked them, 'What things?' They replied: 'Concerning Jesus of Nazareth, who was a prophet mighty in deed and word before God and all the people, and how our chief priests and rulers delivered him up to be condemned to death, and crucified him. But we had hoped he was the one to redeem Israel.

'Yes, and besides all this it is now the third day since this happened. Moreover, some women of our company amazed us. They were at the tomb early in the morning and did not find the body; and they came back saying that they had even seen a vision of angels, who said that he was alive. Some of those who were with us went to the tomb, and found it just as the women has said; but him they did not see.' And he said to them, 'O foolish men, and slow of heart to believe all that the prophets have spoken! Was it not necessary that the Christ should suffer these things and enter into his glory?' And beginning with Moses and all the prophets, he interpreted to them in all the scriptures the things concerning himself. So they drew near to the village to which they were going. He appeared to be going further, but they constrained him saying, 'Stay with us, for it is evening, and the day is now far spent'. So he went in to stay with them. When he was at table with them, he took the bread and blessed, and broke it, and gave it to them. And their eyes were opened and they recognised him; and he vanished out of their sight. They said to each other, 'Did not our hearts burn within us while he talked to us on the road, while he opened to us the scriptures?' And they rose that same hour and returned to Jerusalem; and they found the eleven gathered together and those who were with them, who said, 'The Lord has risen indeed, and has appeared to Simon!' Then they told what had happened on the road, and how he was known to them in the breaking of the bread (Lk 24:13-25). The Breaking of the Bread is the Eucharist.

It is interesting to note that even though Jesus had interpreted for the disciples all that the scriptures had foretold about himself, the disciples did not recognise him until he appeared to them in the Eucharist. 'Then their eyes were opened' and they recognised him 'in the Breaking of the Bread'.

The Apostolic Letter of Pope John Paul II

This Letter is entitled *Mane Nobiscum Domine* ('Stay with us Lord'). It was written for the opening of the Year of the Eucharist, October 2004–October 2005. In this Letter on the Eucharist His Holiness states: 'The image of the disciples on the way to Emmaus can serve as a fitting guide for a year when the Church will be particularly engaged in living out the mystery of the Holy Eucharist ... Through the mystery of his complete hiddenness, Christ becomes a mystery of light ... The Eucharist is light above all because at every Mass the Liturgy of the Word of God precedes the Liturgy of the Eucharist in the unity of the two 'tables', the table of the Word and the table of the bread ... In the account of the disciples on the road to Emmaus, Christ himself intervenes to show, "beginning with Moses and all the prophets", how "all the scriptures" point to the mystery of his person (cf. Lk 24:27). His words make the hearts of the disciples "burn" within them, drawing them out of the darkness of sorrow and despair, and awakening in them a desire to remain with him: "Stay with us, Lord".' (cf. 29)

Pope John Paul also states: 'It is significant that the two disciples on the road to Emmaus, duly prepared by Our Lord's words, recognised him at table through the simple gesture of the "breaking of bread". When minds are enlightened and hearts are enkindled, signs begin to "speak". The Eucharist unfolds in a dynamic context of signs containing a rich and luminous message. Through these signs the mystery in some way opens up before the eyes of the believer.'

Jesus appears to the Apostles in Jerusalem

In the evening of the same day that the two disciples saw Jesus in the breaking of the bread, Jesus stood among the apostles in the upper room of a house in Jerusalem and said to them, 'Peace be with you'. But they were startled and frightened and thought that they saw a spirit. Jesus asked them, 'Why are you troubled, and why do questionings rise in your hearts?' He went on to reassure them, 'See my hands and my feet, that it is I myself; handle me and see; for a spirit has not flesh and bones as you see that I have'. Then he showed them his hands and his feet. To reassure them further he asked, 'Have you anything here to eat?' They gave him a piece of broiled fish, and he took it and ate before them.

The Risen Lord commissions the Apostles to teach all Nations
After his Resurrection Jesus sent word to his apostles that he would meet them in Galilee. So the eleven apostles went to the mountain in Galilee to which he had directed them; there he commissioned them, saying, 'All authority in heaven and on earth has been given to me. Go therefore and make disciples of all nations, baptising them in the name of the Father and of the Son and of the Holy Spirit, teaching them to observe all that I have commanded you; and, lo, I am with you always to the close of the age' (Mt 28:18-20).

By his Passion, Death and Resurrection Jesus has conquered sin, death and hell. He proclaims his divine authority. With this divine authority he commands his apostles to make disciples of all nations, baptising them in the name of the three divine Persons of the Blessed Trinity, the Father and the Son and the Holy Spirit, and teaching the nations to observe all that he had commanded. Jesus gives his authority to the apostles to teach in his name. He will be with them always, helping them in their teaching, and ensuring that the apostles will teach the full truth without any error. Jesus is speaking not only to the apostles, but also to their successors to the close of the age.

*   *   *

THE ASCENSION OF OUR LORD INTO HEAVEN
During forty days after his Resurrection Jesus appeared to his apostles many times, proving to them that he was the Jesus they

knew before his death, and that he had really risen from the dead. He told them not to depart from Jerusalem but to wait for the promise of the Father that before many days they would be baptised with the Holy Spirit. 'He said to them, "You shall receive power when the Holy Spirit has come upon you; and you shall be my witnesses in Jerusalem and in all Judea and Samaria and to the end of the earth". And when he had said this, as they were looking on, he was lifted up, and a cloud took him out of their sight. And while they were gazing into heaven as he went, behold, two men stood by them in white robes, and said, "Men of Galilee, why do you stand looking into heaven? This Jesus, who was taken up from you into heaven, will come in the same way as you saw him go into heaven".' (Acts 1:8-11)

Along with his Death and Resurrection, the Ascension of Jesus is part of the redemptive mystery of our salvation.

After the Consecration in Eucharistic Prayer III of the Mass the Priest says:

> Father, calling to mind the death your Son endured for our salvation,
> his glorious resurrection and ascension into Heaven,
> and ready to greet him when he comes again,
> we offer you in thanksgiving this holy and living sacrifice.
> (The Roman Missal)

* * *

MARY, A 'WOMAN OF THE EUCHARIST'

In his Encyclical Letter, *Ecclesia de Eucharistia*, 'The Church of the Eucharist', Pope John Paul II devotes Chapter VI (53–58) to Mary under the title, 'Woman of the Eucharist'. Since the Church is the Church of the Eucharist, Mary, the Mother of the Church, is rightly called a 'Woman of the Eucharist'. Because of her interior disposition Mary is a Woman of the Eucharist in her whole life. The mystery of the Eucharist is a mystery which calls for complete abandonment to the word of God. Mary's example of faith in God's word is a model for our willingness to believe the word of God on the Eucharist.

There are many solemn occasions in her life when her relationship with the Eucharist is revealed in a special way. At the Annunciation Mary was asked by the angel to believe that the One whom she conceived by the Holy Spirit was the Son of God (Lk 1:30-35). Her faith was expressed in her reply, 'Behold, the handmaid of the Lord; be it done unto me according to thy word'. When she said these words, she made an act of faith in complete abandonment to the word of God.

'Mary conceived the Son of God in the physical reality of his body and blood, anticipating within herself what to some degree happens sacramentally in every believer who receives, under the signs of bread and wine, the Lord's body and blood.' (para. 55)

Other Titles given to Mary – (From Vatican II)
'In her maternal charity Mary cares for the brethren of her Son who still journey on earth surrounded by dangers and difficulties, until they are led to their happy fatherland. Therefore, the Blessed Virgin is invoked by the Church under the titles of Advocate, Auxiliatrix, Adjutrix and Mediatrix. These, however, are to be so understood that they neither take away from nor add anything to the dignity and efficacy of Christ the one Mediator.' (*The Church*, 62)

*   *   *

THE BOOK OF REVELATION
The Book of Revelation was written about AD 95 by St John the Evangelist, while he was in exile on the island of Patmos during the persecution of Christians by the Roman Emperor Domician. Because of the persecution it was a time of great suffering for the scattered Christian communities. The immediate purpose of the book was to offer consolation and encouragement to those Christians who were being persecuted at the time John was writing, but ultimately the book was intended for Christians of all places

and times as an instruction on the eschatology of the Christian Church.

The Book of Revelation is the final book in the New Testament. Though little known generally, it is a book of great significance in the scheme of divine Revelation. Here we get a glimpse of the final home of the pilgrim people of God, the reward of all their labours, the fulfilment of all human aspirations, the final destiny of God's people in the eternal happiness of heaven.

The greater part of the book is taken up with a description of a vision of heaven. As well as the vision of heaven there are detailed descriptions of several successive scenes, some portraying life in heaven, others relating to conditions on earth. Because of the persecutions, and because of the atrocities committed in the old pagan Roman empire, the descriptions of the pervading evil can be bewildering for readers; nevertheless, the final result is the triumph of good over evil. The burden of the message of the vision of heaven is that the Church in accordance with God's plan makes its way through human history, suffering opposition, persecution and countless trials towards its final destiny, its fulfilment as the New Jerusalem.

The Heavenly Liturgy and the Earthly Liturgy

Our aim here is to concentrate on the descriptions of the Liturgy in heaven and the Liturgy of the Church on earth. Essentially the two liturgies are the same. The places of celebration are different. The people taking part are different; in the earthly liturgy the people participating are the faithful on earth, not yet perfect but on the way to perfection; in the heavenly liturgy the people participating are the saints in heaven; they have achieved the perfection planned by Almighty God. 'When the perfect comes, the imperfect will pass away ... For now we see in a mirror dimly, but then face to face.' (1 Cor 13:10, 12)

The Liturgy of the Eucharist in Heaven

In the earthly liturgy of the Eucharist there are many references to the Liturgy of the Eucharist in heaven. In the Book of Revelation

John describes his vision of heaven. What now follows are some of his descriptions:

Worship of God the Father
'At once I was in the Spirit, and lo, a throne stood in heaven, with one seated on the throne!' (Rev 4:1-2). Around the throne stood twenty-four elders, representing the Old and the New Testaments; these and many other groups who took part in the service of praising God never ceased to sing, 'Holy, holy, holy, is the Lord God Almighty, who was and is and is to come! ... Worthy art thou, our Lord and God, to receive glory and honour and power, for thou didst create all things, and by thy will they existed and were created' (Rev 4:8-11).

Worship of God the Son, the Lamb
John describes his vision of the Lamb in heaven: 'And between the throne and the four living creatures and among the elders I saw a Lamb standing, as though it had been slain, with seven horns and seven eyes which are the seven spirits of God sent out into all the earth.' Then those present fell down before the Lamb, each holding a harp and bowls full of incense. They sang a new song, saying:
'Worthy art thou to take the scroll and to open its seals, for thou wast slain and by thy blood didst ransom men for God from every tribe and tongue and people and nation.' (Rev 5:6, 9)
    The voices of many angels numbering myriads of myriads, and thousands of thousands joined in the adoration of the Lamb. The 'Lamb standing' signifies the crucified Christ risen from the dead. The music and singing and the use of incense signify the liturgical character of the celebration in heaven. The sealed scroll contained God's plan for the world.

Worship of God the Father and God the Son, the Lamb
'And I heard every creature in heaven and on earth and under the earth and in the sea, and all therein, saying, "To him who sits upon the throne and to the Lamb be blessing and honour and glory and

might for ever and ever". And the four living creatures said, "Amen!", and the elders fell down and worshipped.' (Rev 5:13-14)

The adoration given equally to the Father and the Son shows that the divine Persons of the Blessed Trinity are equal in their divinity.

The Holy Spirit

Water is a symbol of the Holy Spirit. The water of baptism symbolises our birth into the divine life (Jn 4:13-14). 'The origin and growth of the Church are symbolised by the blood and water which flowed from the open side of the crucified Jesus.' (*The Church,* 3)

The Holy Spirit proceeds from the Father and the Son

Then he who talked to John 'showed me the river of the water of life bright as crystal, flowing from the throne of God the Father and of the Lamb through the middle of the street of the city; also on either side of the river, the tree of life, its twelve kinds of fruit, yielding its fruit each month; and the leaves of the tree for the healing of the nations' (Rev 21:1-2).

The Holy Spirit gives a share in the divine life to those who receive him, and all the accompanying gifts and fruits that overflow in abundance from the spiritual river into every nation.

The Holy Spirit, the third Person of the Blessed Trinity, proceeds from the Father and the Son. The Father and the Son send the Holy Spirit on the apostles and on the newly launched Church.

The Woman Clothed with the Sun

'And a great portent appeared in heaven, a woman clothed with the sun, with the moon under her feet, and on her head a crown of twelve stars.' (Rev 12:1) In the Book of Genesis (3:15) the woman promised by God to be the Mother of the Redeemer was Mary the Mother of Jesus. Jesus addressed his Mother as 'Woman' at the wedding feast of Cana and when he was dying on the cross. The Woman clothed with the sun seen in the vision of heaven was Mary the Mother of Jesus. As her Son was King of heaven and earth, Mary was Queen of heaven and earth. In heaven Mary leads all the angels and saints in the liturgical adoration, thanks and praise given to God, Father, Son and Holy Spirit. On earth she has given adoration, thanks and praise to God in her Magnificat.

Identical Characteristics of the Heavenly and Earthly Liturgies

Worship of the three divine Persons of the Blessed Trinity is central to the heavenly Liturgy. Special worship is given to Jesus, the Lamb, because he redeemed the world by his Passion, Death, Resurrection and Ascension.

In the earthly liturgy, the liturgy of the Eucharist, the hymn 'Glory to God in the Highest' is proclaimed or sung in adoration, thanks and praise to each of the divine Persons; to God the Father, the priest and people say, 'Lord God, heavenly King, almighty God and Father, we worship you, we give you thanks, we praise you for your glory'. Nearly all of the remainder of the hymn is addressed to God the Son: 'Lord Jesus Christ, only Son of the Father, Lord God, Lamb of God, you take away the sin of the world, have mercy on us.' The last verse is addressed to Jesus Christ and the Holy Spirit: 'You alone are the Most High, Jesus Christ, with the Holy Spirit in the glory of God the Father.'

The Creed – The Profession of Faith

In the Creed the priest and people profess their faith in each of the three divine Persons in one God. The Creed is more than an act of faith; it is also an expression of joy in the gift of faith, and of thanks and praise to God for all the mighty works performed by God for the salvation of the world. Again the greater part of the Creed is devoted to the life, death and Resurrection of Jesus Christ the Redeemer.

The Preface to the Eucharistic Prayer

The Preface to the Eucharistic Prayer in the Mass combines characteristics from both the earthly and the heavenly liturgies; it ends with the acclamation: 'Now with angels and archangels, and the whole company of heaven, we sing the unending hymn of your praise:

> Holy, holy, holy, Lord God of power and might,
> heaven and earth are full of your glory,
> Hosanna in the highest,
> Blessed is he who comes in the name of the Lord,
> Hosanna in the highest.

At the beginning of Eucharistic Prayer III the priest celebrant invokes the three divine Persons: 'Father, you are holy indeed, and all creation rightly gives you praise. All life, all holiness comes from you through your Son Jesus Christ, our Lord, by the working of the Holy Spirit.' After the Consecration of the Eucharist, at the end of the Eucharistic Prayer, the priest celebrant proclaims, 'We hope to enjoy for ever the vision of your glory, through Christ our Lord, from whom all good things come'.

> Through him, with him, in him, in the unity of the Holy Spirit,
> all glory and honour is yours almighty Father,
> for ever and ever.

At the beginning of the Mass the priest celebrant makes the sign of the cross, the symbol of the sacrifice of the Lamb, while invoking the three divine Persons, in the name of the Father, and of the Son and of the Holy Spirit. The Mass concludes with the Blessing of the People by the priest who makes the sign of the cross over the people, saying, 'May Almighty God bless you, the Father, the Son and the Holy Spirit'.

The Scroll

The scroll with its seven seals contained God's designs kept secret until the breaking of the seals. Listening to the reading of these designs led the people to praise God. In the liturgy of the Word in the celebration of Mass, reading the scriptures leads the people to worship God.

Music and Singing, Incense and Vestments

In both the earthly liturgy and the heavenly liturgy there is much use of sacred music and hymns, incense and liturgical vestments. These enhance the spiritual joy of the worship of God on earth and in heaven.

The Eucharistic Prayer of the Earthly Liturgy

At the centre of the Eucharistic Prayer in the Mass are the words spoken by Jesus Christ, when he instituted the Eucharist at the Last Supper. By the words of consecration Jesus changed bread and wine into his body and blood. The Real Presence of Jesus in the Eucharist is veiled under the sacramental signs of bread and wine, that is, under the appearance of food. Jesus is to be consumed as food in the Eucharist in order to form a close intimate union between himself and his Church: 'He who eats my flesh and drinks my blood abides in me and I in him.' This intimate union between Jesus and each member of his Church is, for each, a 'foretaste of heaven'.

The Eucharist as food under the signs of bread and wine was part of God's plan from the beginning. The Eucharist as food was prefigured in many different ways in the Old Testament; the Eucharist at the Last Supper fulfilled the many and varied revelations of the past.

The New and Everlasting Covenant

At the consecration of the wine at the Last Supper, Jesus said, 'This is the cup of my blood, the blood of the New and Everlasting Covenant'. The New and Everlasting Covenant is the Covenant of Love, between Jesus Christ and his Church. It is the Covenant of the Eucharist. The last words of Jesus on the cross were, 'It is finished'. After that 'he bowed his head and gave up his spirit'. Later when the soldiers came to break his legs, they saw that he was already dead. 'But one of the soldiers pierced his side with a spear, and at once there came out blood and water.' This pouring out of the last drop of Jesus Christ's blood on the cross was the ratification of the New and Everlasting Covenant between Jesus Christ and his Church, the Covenant of the Eucharist, the inauguration of the Church on earth.

In heaven the Covenant of the Eucharist is perfected, and becomes the celebration of the Marriage of the Lamb and the Marriage Feast of the Lamb (cf. *CCC*, p. 1402).

The Marriage of the Lamb

The mystical marriage of the Lamb was foreshadowed in the Old Testament: 'Tradition has always seen in the Song of Soloman a unique expression of human love, a pure reflection of God's love, "a love strong as death", that many waters cannot quench.' (CCC, p. 1611) The Covenant of Sinai between God and his people had prepared the way for the New Covenant of the Last Supper. This New Covenant was perfected in heaven in the Marriage of the Lamb (cf. *CCC*, p. 1612). Some of the prophets had foreshadowed the mystical marriage. The prophet Isaias wrote:

> I will greatly rejoice in the Lord,
> my soul shall exult in my God;
> for he has clothed me with the garments of salvation,
> he has covered me with the robe of righteousness,
> as a bridegroom decks himself with a garland
> and as a bride adorns herself with her jewels …
> For as a young man marries a virgin,
> so shall your sons marry you
> and as the bridegroom rejoices over the bride,
> so shall your God rejoice over you.
> (Isa 61:10; 62:5)

Recorded in the Book of Revelation

In the Book of Revelation St John describes the Marriage of the

Lamb and the Marriage Supper of the Lamb. The Lamb is Jesus Christ the Redeemer; the Bride of the Lamb is the Church, the New Jerusalem:

> Then I heard what seemed to be the voice of a great multitude,
> like the sound of many waters and like the sound of mighty thunder peals, crying,
> 'Hallelujah! For the Lord our God the Almighty reigns,
> let us rejoice and exult and give him the glory,
> for the Marriage of the Lamb has come,
> and his Bride has made herself ready;
> it was granted her to be clothed with fine linen, bright and pure' –
> for the fine linen is the righteous deeds of the saints.
> And the angel said to me, 'Write this: Blessed are those who are invited to the Marriage Supper of the Lamb'.
> (Rev 19:6-9)

The Marriage of the Lamb – The Perfect Union of Jesus with His Church

In suffering his Passion and Death Jesus gave himself to be crucified out of love for his Church; in Holy Communion he gives himself in an intimate union of love with his Church; Jesus had promised this union with his Church, when he said, 'He who eats my flesh and drinks my blood abides in me, and I in him' (Jn 6:56). In the Marriage of the Lamb in heaven, Jesus gives himself eternally in the perfect, intimate union of love with his Church. The veil of sacramental signs is removed; the redeemed see Jesus face to face. Jesus forms an intimate, direct union between his crucified, risen and glorified body and the whole redeemed Church in heaven, and with each individual, glorified member of the Church. The heavenly liturgy perfects the earthly liturgy (cf. *CCC*, p. 1136).

Blessed are those who are invited to the Marriage Feast of the Lamb
The perfect joy and eternal rejoicing that come from union with Jesus Christ in heaven is the eternal Marriage Feast of the Lamb.

The New Heaven and the New Earth
St John describes the vision: 'Then I saw a new heaven and a new earth; for the first heaven and the first earth had passed away, and the sea was no more. And I saw the Holy City, new Jerusalem, coming down out of heaven from God, prepared as a bride adorned for her husband; and I heard a great voice from the throne saying, "Behold, the dwelling of God is with men. He will dwell with them, and they shall be his people, and God himself will be with them; he will wipe every tear from their eyes, and death shall be no more, neither shall there be mourning nor crying nor pain any more, for the former things have passed away". And he who sat upon the throne said, "Behold, I make all things new". Also he said, "Write this, for these words are trustworthy and true". And he said to me, "It is done! I am the Alpha and the Omega, the beginning and the end".' (Rev 21:1-6)

The material universe is also destined to be transformed and restored to its original state to be at the service of the redeemed sharing their glorification in the risen Jesus Christ (cf. *CCC*, pp. 1042–47).

The Holy City, the New Jerusalem
The Holy City, the New Jerusalem is the redeemed Church in heaven; the redeemed Church is the Bride of the Lamb. 'Then came one of the seven angels who … spoke to me, saying, "Come, I will show you the Bride, the wife of the Lamb". And in the spirit he carried me away to a great, high mountain, and showed me the holy city Jerusalem coming down out of heaven from God, having the glory of God, its radiance like a most rare jewel, like a jasper, clear as crystal.' (Rev 21:9-11) 'But nothing unclean shall enter it, nor any one who practises abomination or falsehood, but only those who are written in the Lamb's book of life.' (Rev 21:27)

Appendix

Homily of Pope John Paul II on the Apparition at Knock
On 'Laetare' Sunday, 13 March, the Holy Father addressed the pilgrims gathered in St Peter's Square for the recitation of the 'Angelus', continuing his series of spiritual pilgrimages to Marian shrines throughout the world on the occasion of the Marian Year:

1. The goal of our spiritual pilgrimage today is the Marian shrine at Knock in Ireland, the land of that great apostle St Patrick, whose liturgical memorial we shall celebrate this coming Thursday.

   The Lord granted me to visit that sanctuary so dear to the Irish people, on 30 September 1979, during my pastoral visit in that beloved nation of deep Christian traditions. My visit coincided with the celebration of the first centenary of the apparition of Our Lady, Queen of Ireland, with St Joseph and St John the Apostle, on the southern wall of the humble parish church of the village of Knock, in a rural area in the western part of the country. From that day on, 21 August 1879, Knock has become a place of pilgrimage and a point of reference for the deep-rooted Marian devotion of the Irish people.

2. Two aspects of the apparition of Knock attract our attention. First of all, the apparition lasted long enough to allow the first persons who, passing near the little village church, saw the

heavenly figures, to go and call the inhabitants of the houses scattered throughout the countryside; thus about eighteen persons in all, men, women and young people, were witnesses to the event.

Second, there were no words spoken during the apparition at Knock. Mary Most Holy had a golden crown on her head – Queen of Peace – and her hands were raised in an attitude of supplication; by their gestures, she and the other heavenly protagonists of the apparition invite us to prayer, to meditate on the sacred scriptures, to reconciliation with God obtained by Christ, the Lamb that was slain for our ransom. Indeed, characteristic elements of the pilgrimages to Knock, where in 1976 a new church was dedicated to welcome the growing number of visitors, have been prayer, especially the Rosary, penance and sacramental reconciliation, as well as the blessing of the sick.

3. I invite all who are listening to me to pray with me to Our Lady of Knock, Queen of Peace, for the beloved land of Ireland, that her people may always remain faithful to their Christian vocation which has so deeply permeated her history. I invite you to pray that the political violence and terrorism which has been causing death and suffering for twenty years now in the Catholic and Protestant communities, may come to an end in that land of St Patrick.

Today I repeat the words which I addressed to the Blessed Virgin on the occasion of my visit to the sanctuary of Knock:

'Queen of Ireland, Mary Mother of the heavenly and earthly Church, "a Mháthair Dé", keep Ireland true to her spiritual tradition and her Christian heritage. Help her to respond to her historic mission of bringing the light of Christ to the nations … We entrust to your motherly care the land of Ireland, where you have been and are so much loved. Help this land to stay true to you and your Son always'.[1]

Notes

Chapter 2

1. The text is in fact from Mark, Chapter 11.

Chapter 4

1. The sources for this chapter are the following:
    A. Poulain, SJ, *The Graces of Interior Prayer*, translated from the French by Leonora L., Yorke Smith; London, Routledge & Kegan Paul Ltd., 1928; cc. XX–XXIII.
    Mgr Albert Farges, *Mystical Phenomena*, London, Burns Oates, 1926, Part II, c.1.
    A. Tanquerey, *The Spiritual Life*, Desclee & Co., Tournai, Part II, Book III c. III.
    J. Maréchal, SJ, *Studies in the Psychology of the Mystics*, London, Burns Oates, pp. 102–110.
2. *Summa* III, q.76, a.8
3. A. Poulain, p. 302.
4. Ibid.
5. A. Poulain, p. 353.
6. *De Serv. Dei Beatific*, Translation from Tanquerey, p. 701.
7. *Acta Apostolicae Sedis*, 11, 1877.

Chapter 5

1. MacPhilpin, *The Apparitions and Miracles at Knock*, p. 29.
2. T.D. Sullivan, *Apparition at the Church at Knock*, p. 21.
3. MacPhilpin, p. 29.
4. T.D. Sullivan, pp. 21–2.
5. Cf. Catherine Rynne, *Knock 1879–1979*, Appendix 3, Veritas Publications, Dublin, 1979.

Chapter 7

1. Liam Ua Cadhain, *Knock Shrine,* 1935, pp. 53–5.
2. The original is preserved in the Acts of the 1936 Commission, Tuam Diocesan Archive.
3. MacPhilpin, p. 15.
4. The original statements of the last three of the twelve statements published by T.D. Sullivan in the *Weekly News,* February 1880, were discovered in a box containing the Cusack Papers in the archive of the Sisters of Peace, Washington, USA. Sister Mary Francis Cusack (the Nun of Kenmare) was the founder of the Congregation of the Sisters of Peace in the USA. The last three of the depositions published in the *Weekly News* are exactly the same as the three originals discovered in Washington except for a few words which do not change the meaning of the depositions. The last three depositions of the *Weekly News* correspond with the twelfth, thirteenth and fourteenth depositions published by MacPhilpin. Along with the depositions discovered in the Cusack Papers were letters giving information on miraculous cures claimed at Knock Shrine. All the papers dealing with the apparition at Knock were given in 1998 by the Sisters of Peace, Washington, USA, to Knock Shrine Archive, Knock, Co. Mayo.

Chapter 8

1. MacPhilpin, p. 15.
2. *Beauraing and Other Apparitions,* pp. 125, 127; London, Burns Oates, 1934.
3. T.D. Sullivan, pp. 12–13.
4. She stated later that she did not know it had already been locked by her sister.
5. pp. 53–5.
6. MacPhilpin, p. 29.
7. T.D. Sullivan, pp. 4–5.
8. MacPhilpin, pp. 54–5, quoting from the *Daily Telegraph.*
9. MacPhilpin, pp. 25–6, quoting from the *Daily Telegraph.*
10. Liam Ua Cadhain, *Knock Shrine,* 1935.
11. The method of inquiry followed from here to the end of this chapter is based largely on the method outlined and explained by Mgr Albert Farges, *Mystical Phenomena,* pp. 350–401.
12. Joseph Maréchal, SJ, *Studies in the Psychology of the Mystics,* p. 64 (quoting J. Seglas).
13. Farges, op. cit., p. 399.
14. Commentators are agreed that both the mediation of Jesus Christ and

the mediation of Mary the Mother of Jesus are symbolised in the apparition. There is no doubt which of the two is the more important, but the question here is on which of the two is attention being focused in the apparition. The opinion that Mary's mediation is the principal message enjoys the greater favour. The considerations which support this view are: (1) The witnesses were attracted most of all by the figure of Mary the Mother of Jesus. (2) The faithful have always regarded the apparition as an apparition of Our Lady. (3) While the altar, lamb and cross were described by the witnesses as being at the centre of the gable, and on a higher level than the figures, they were nevertheless said to be behind the figures.

15. Poulain, p. 299.
16. MacPhilpin, p. 58.
17. 1936 Commission, Tuam Diocesan Archive.
18. Poulain, p. 353.
19. Poulain, p. 302.
20. Sr M.F. Cusack, *Three Visits to Knock*, p. 61.
21. Poulain, pp. 349–50; Farges, p. 387.

Chapter 9
1. Quoted by MacPhilpin, pp. 61–2, from *Daily Telegraph*.
2. T.D. Sullivan, pp. 8–9 (extracts).
3. pp. 98–106.
4. The reference is to the Convent of Mercy, Claremorris.
5. *Weekly News*, 11 August 1883. Quoted from W.D. Coyne, *Our Lady of Knock*, pp. 106–7.
6. *Knock Shrine*, p. 54.

Chapter 10
1. Farges, pp. 401–2.
2. T.D. Sullivan, pp. 16–19.
3. T.D. Sullivan, pp. 24–5.
4. MacPhilpin, pp. 51–2.
5. MacPhilpin, p. 53.
6. Farges, pp. 401–2.
7. MacPhilpin's second edition of his book in 1894 gives a brief description of the January–February occurrences; he distinguishes clearly between the apparition of 1879 and the occurrences of 1880.
8. Tuam Diocesan Archive.
9. Cf. Warren, pp. 14–16, quoted from the *Irish Times*.
10. pp. 18–20.

Chapter 11

1.   MacPhilpin, p. 59.
2.   T.D. Sullivan, p. 6.
3.   T.D. Sullivan, p. 28.

Chapter 13

1.   First Autobiography, Sr Mary Francis Cusack, p. 193.

Sr Mary Francis Cusack had been a member of an Anglican Community of Sisters in London. On her reception into the Catholic Church she entered the Poor Clare Convent in Newry, Co. Down in 1859. In October 1861 she came, along with other Sisters, to make a new foundation in Kenmare. While she was in Kenmare she attained international fame through her writings on political and social matters and also through her charitable work during a period of famine; her organisation to help the poor was called the 'Nun of Kenmare Distress Fund'. She visited Knock in November 1881, and in 1882 she received permission, on certain conditions from Archbishop McEvilly of Tuam, to found a convent in Knock. While in Knock she published the book, *Three Visits to Knock*. Disagreements later arose between herself and the Church authorities about her plans for Knock. In 1883 she received at her own request a transfer from Tuam Diocese to Nottingham, England, where she established a new religious order. In 1884 she opened a new foundation in New Jersey, USA. Her request to open a foundation in New York was refused. This led to some controversy. Eventually she left her religious order and returned to England and to the Anglican Communion. She wrote a second autobiography.

Recent research by Sr Catherine Ferguson, CSJP, Newry, Co. Down, discovered new unpublished evidence which shows that Archbishop McEvilly and Archdeacon Cavanagh were reasonable and fair in their dealings with Sr Mary Francis Cusack. The evidence also shows that she claimed to have seen visions of Our Lord and Our Lady, when she was in Kenmare. Her descriptions of the visions are not convincing. Her association with Knock was short.

Chapter 14

1.   For the personal experience which influenced Dr Gilmartin's decision to attend the devotions at Knock on the fiftieth anniversary of the apparition, see *Providence my Guide* by Judy Coyne, pp. 110–1, Mercier Press, 2004.
2.   *Knock Shrine Annual*, 1953.

Chapter 15
1. Quoted from *Knock Shrine Annual*, 1951, pp. 10–12.
2. Quoted from Liam Ua Cadhain, *Knock Shrine*, 1949, p. 326.
3. Cf. *Places Apart, Knock* by Eileen Good, Veritas Publications, Dublin, 2002; *Reflecting at Knock* by Thomas Lane, CM, Columba Press, Dublin, 2007.
4. For the spiritual favours granted by the Holy See to Knock Shrine, for the Visit of His Holiness Pope John Paul II and for developments in the Knock Shrine area, see *The Glory of Knock*, by Mgr Michael Walsh, published by the Custodians of Knock Shrine.

Chapter 16
1. Cf. Scott Hahn, *The Lamb's Supper*.
2. Cf. Pope John Paul II, *Ecclesia de Eucharistia*, Chapter VI, CTS, London, 2003.

Chapter 17
1. Taken from www.vatican.va/holyfather/benedictxvl/homilies/2005. Accessed on 1 September 2007.
2. Cf. *Way of the Cross*, by G. Cyprian Alston, OSB, Vol. XV, Catholic Encyclopaedia, London and New York, R. Appleton Co., 1912.
3. Cf. *Veronica* by Antoine Degert, Vol. XV, Robert Appleton Company, London, New York, 1909, 1912.
4. For the order in the events after the Resurrection cf. *The Lord*, part VI, by Romano Guardini, Henry Regency Co., Chicago, IL, 1954.

Appendix
1. Quoted from *L'Osservatore Romano*, 21 March 1988.

Bibliography

The evidence for the apparition at Knock is contained chiefly in the reports of the two Ecclesiastical Commissions of 1879 and 1936. The Report of the former Commission was published in John MacPhilpin's work. The original documents of the latter Commission are in the Tuam Diocesan archives. The following is a list of authors whose published works were consulted for the first, second and third editions of this book:

John MacPhilpin, *The Apparitions and Miracles at Knock*, M.H. Gill & Son, Dublin, 1880.

T.D. Sullivan, *Apparitions at the Church of Knock*, Dublin, 1880.

C.P. Warren, *The Apparitions of Our Blessed Lady at Knock*, Dublin, 1880.

Liam Ua Cadhain (William D. Coyne), *Knock Shrine*, O'Gorman, Galway, 1935.

– *Cnoc Mhuire (Knock Shrine) in Picture and Story*, O'Gorman, Galway, 1945.

– *Our Lady of Knock*, Catholic Publishing Co., New York, 1948.

– *Venerable Archdeacon Cavanagh*, Knock Shrine Society, 1953.

Rev. Michael O'Carroll, CSSp, *The Secret of Knock*, The Holy Ghost Fathers, Dublin, 1941.

Rev. Fr Hubert, OFM Cap, T*he Grace of Knock*, Cecil Paul Hurwitz Publications, Cork, 1951.

John Beevers, *The Sun her Mantle* (especially chapter headed 'The Silent Figures'), Browne & Nolan, Dublin, 1953.

Eileen Good, *Places Apart, Knock*, Veritas, Dublin, 2002.

Thomas Lane CM, *Reflecting at Knock*, Columba, Dublin, 2007.

The following authors were consulted for the mystical and psychological aspects of apparitions:

Rev. A. Poulain, SJ, *The Graces of Interior Prayer*, Routledge and Kegan Paul, London, 1928.

Mgr Albert Farges, *Mystical Phenomena*, Burns Oates and Washbourne, London, 1926.

Rev. A. Tanquerey, *The Spiritual Life*, Desclee & Co., Tournai, 1939.

Rev. J. Marechal, SJ, *Studies in the Psychology of the Mystics*, Burns Oates & Washbourne, London, 1927.

Rev. H. Thurston, SJ, *Beauraing and Other Apparitions*, Burns Oates & Washbourne, London, 1934.

Sources used for the Scriptural Meaning of the Apparitions:

The Holy Bible, Revised Standard Version Catholic Edition, Ignatius Press, San Francisco, 1966.

The Navarre Bible, Pentateuch, Gospels and Acts, Letters, Texts and Commentaries, Four Courts Press, Dublin; Scepter Publishers, Princeton NJ, 1999.

The Documents of Vatican II, Walter Abbott, SJ, The American Press, Geoffrey Chapman, London, Dublin, 1966.

The Catechism of the Catholic Church, Veritas, Dublin, 1994.

Letter of Pope John Paul II to the Bishops: On the Mystery and Worship of the Holy Eucharist, CTS, London, 1980.

Encyclical Letter, *Ecclesia de Eucharistia*, CTS, London, 2003.

Apostolic Letter, *Mane Nobiscum Domine* (Stay with us Lord), For the Year of the Eucharist, October 2004–October 2005.

God is Near Us, The Eucharist the Heart of Life, Joseph Cardinal Ratzinger, Ignatius Press, San Francisco, 2003.

Pope Benedict XVI, *Homily During Mass on World Youth Day*, Cologne, 21 August 2005, Libreria Editrice Vaticana, www.vatican.va.

The Book of Psalms, Vol. 1, Psalm 22 (1953), *The Book of Psalms*, Vol. II, Psalm 117 (118), Kissane, Browne & Nolan Ltd., Richview Press, Dublin, 1954.

The Lamb's Supper, Scott Hahn, Doubleday House Inc., New York 1999; *Hail, Holy Queen*, Scott Hahn, Doubleday, New York, 2001.

The Lord, Romano Guardini, Henry Regnery Company, Chicago, IL, 1954.

The Catholic Encyclopaedia, 'Eucharist: Transubstantiation: Christ assumes a new, sacramental mode of being', Vol.V; 'Way of the Cross', Vol. XV, by Cyprian Alston OSB; *Veronica*, Vol. XV, by Antoine Degert, Toulouse, Robert Appleton Company, London, New York, 1909, 1912.